CURSING AND CROSSING

HOODOO SPELLS TO TORMENT, JINX, AND TAKE REVENGE ON YOUR ENEMIES

MISS AIDA

Lucky Mojo Curio Company
Forestville, California

→ 2017 ←

Cursing and Crossing:
Hoodoo Spells to Torment, Jinx, and Take Revenge on Your Enemies
by Miss Aida

Text:
K. Aida Severini, MS, BSN, RN; catherine yronwode

Editor:
catherine yronwode

Cover:
Greywolf Townsend, Unknown Artist

Art:
Charles M. Quinlan, Charles C. Dawson, K. Rudin, charlie wiley,
Jean-Baptiste Alliette [Etteilla], Oswald Wirth, nagasiva yronwode,
catherine yronwode, Unknown Artists, and Greywolf Townsend

Typesetting:
catherine yronwode

Production:
nagasiva yronwode, Charles Porterfield

First Edition 2017
Second Edition 2017

Published by
The Lucky Mojo Curio Company
6632 Covey Road
Forestville, California 95436
LuckyMojo.com

ISBN: 978-0-9961471-5-6

Printed in Canada.

CONTENTS

DEDICATION

To all my loves: Kiriaki Catel, Nick Catel, Virgen Caridad del Cobre, Mama Oshun, Papa Oggun, Mama Oya, Papa Babalu-Aye, Princess Athena XVII, Lobo vom Hexenmeister, all the Santos, Orishas, Archangels, Spirit Guides, Guardian Angels, my Eggun, and my little angels: Athena's Asha vom Atlas, Lobo Junior von Hexenmeister, Athena's Wolfgang vom Atlas, and Ariel the Pookie-Bird.

ACKNOWLEDGEMENTS

I would like to thank the following for their contributions:

First and foremost, catherine yronwode has been my teacher, mentor, friend, and colleague for years — and now she is my editor. Catherine is the epitome of kindness and humbleness. Thank you, catherine, for being in my life and for being you. You are truly a gift from God.

Ana Patterson, Professor Charles Porterfield, and nagasiva yronwode have worked hard to help me write this book, tolerating my endless questions with both patience and kindness. I really don't think I could have finished this project without them.

Greywolf Townsend, my art director, has made this somewhat forbidding volume attractive, for which I am very grateful.

My padrinos in both Santeria and Palo taught me so very much: not only about magic, but also about life. They were classy, honourable people. I am forever grateful to them for having been in my life, and I am sure that they were watching over me as I wrote this book.

Thank you to the Lucky Mojo Forum members who have been like my own family. Thank you for all that you have taught me.

And a special thank you to my loyal clients, whom I love as if they were my own children, sisters, and brothers. I love you!

Finally, my thanks go out to those who have contributed to this book: Susan Barnes, Candelo Kimbisa, Catherine Yronwode, Deacon Millett, Troll Towelhead (Grand Mufti of Satanism), Professor Ames, Dr. Johannes, Nathan Steininger, Professor Charles Porterfield, Ms. Robin, Apollo Dark, Briana Saussy, and the Reverend Harry M. Hyatt's 1,600 generous and knowledgeable informants — thank you for your fantastic spells!

HOODOO, CONJURE, ROOTWORK

WHAT HOODOO IS

When people buy a spell-book, they often assume that the magical practices described are universal, and that all sorcerers know these secrets. The truth is quite different. Magic always develops in specific geographical regions and among people of specific cultures. To put it simply, Indonesian folk magic is not the same as Apache folk magic; the supplies used and the social situations for which help is sought vary by culture.

Hoodoo, also known as conjure, tricking, rootwork, or helping yourself, is a form of folk magic with deep roots in the ancient cultures of Central and West Africa, the regions from which most African slaves were brought to North America. African ways of working remain the core of this work, but with African roots and herbs not available, Native American and European curios have long been substituted. Likewise, as enslaved Africans became Christians, prayers to African deities were replaced with Christian prayers.

Each colonial power claimed its own region of Africa. The cultures of Africans under Portuguese or Spanish rule were different than those under English or French rule. These differences continued in the Americas, and further divergences were introduced when the people enslaved by English families became Protestants, and those enslaved by French, Spanish, and Portuguese families became Catholics. After Emancipation, black Americans freely experimented with and adopted ideas from other cultures, and for this reason we also see fragments of Jewish, Irish, German, Spanish, and Chinese beliefs and spells incorporated into hoodoo.

WHAT HOODOO IS NOT

African diasporic religions like Voodoo, Santeria, Palo, and Quimbanda retain African pantheons of deities, sometimes combined with Catholic saints. They are initiatic and although their clerics may practice magic, their chief aim is to venerate their pantheons.

African diasporic folk magic traditions like Jamaican obeah and American hoodoo are forms of folk magic, and thus their major aim is to help people gain power over situations and other people.

INTRODUCTION

IDENTIFYING OUR ENEMIES

Sometimes, people can be so heartless and evil in their intentions and actions. They don't care whom they hurt. Rather than looking at innocent people and considering the potential consequences to them, they instead look through their victims, as if they are insignificant pieces of garbage.

Below is a brief list of those who embody EVIL. In our lifetimes, most of us have met or have fallen victim to at least one type of oppressor:

- **The Bullies:** They act out aggressive behaviours against those whom they perceive as weaker or smaller than themselves for no logical reason other than to assert their power upon their victims.
- **The Thieves:** They steal what their victims have worked hard to establish or acquire, such as their happy relationships, their friends, their money, their prestige, their livelihood, or their material possessions.
- **The Liars, Con Artists, and Scammers:** They employ verbal and physical ruses, including plagiarism, sleight of hand, and forgery to gain trust, so that they can take money or gifts under false pretences.
- **The Jealous and Envious Ones:** Not stealing for personal gain, they instead spoil and lay waste the lives of anybody who embodies a skill or represents a place in life that they cannot achieve themselves.
- **The Spouse and Child Abusers:** They engage in the personal torture of family victims through threats, violence, imprisonment, unsanitary living conditions, rape, and the withholding of food or health care.
- **The Animal Abusers:** They select victims from among other species, and subject them to physical torture, imprisonment, unsanitary living conditions, and the withholding of food or health care.
- **The Sociopaths and Psychopaths:** Amoral and conscienceless, they seek immediate gratification at any cost, saying and doing whatever is necessary to gain their own immediate satisfaction.

These are the people who stop at nothing. Even getting caught is not likely to deter them from their wicked ways. They are the selfish and self-serving predators found in every society and every culture. And, unfortunately, they have existed since the beginning of recorded history.

WHY WE CURSE

We know that evil people have lived among us for thousands of years. Even Psalms 37 of the Bible describes them: *"The wicked plotteth against the just, and gnashes upon him with his teeth ... The wicked watches the righteous and seeketh to slay him."* What did our ancient ancestors do to seek revenge against the wicked?

When society and the legal systems failed these victims, some got revenge by injuring or killing their oppressors in retaliation for the injustices done to them or their families. Others sought the assistance of professional henchmen to harm or kill their tormentors. And the clever ones prayed and implemented magical curses for their revenge.

Archæologists have uncovered thousands of ancient artifacts that embodied magical curses of revenge. Those inscribed on clay or into thin sheets of metal are known as curse tablets, defixiones, or katedesmoi; those made in the form of dolls or drawings are referred to as tortured effigies. You, dear reader, are very likely the descendant of someone who knew how to curse; we all are, most probably.

Sadly, times have not much changed since our forebears were combatting injustice. The wicked often prevail through force or by rigging the legal system, and society often ignores our torment with attitudes of apathy.

Personally, there have been times that I would have loved to have hired a professional hit man to inflict severe physical injury on my tormentors — and I would have loved to have watched and cheered on my beloved henchman as he did it! But in the end I also know that we must all abide by our own ethical standards, our culture's moral codes, and the legal laws of our land, because otherwise, we are no better than our oppressors.

So, although easier said than done, it's better to walk away from a provocative experience rather than to put myself in either a legal or physically dangerous situation. Yes, I have been known to throw a mean punch here and there, but, through luck, and luck only, I was not incarcerated for my actions — and, most fortunately, my mother, as well as most of my family, were magical practitioners who taught me what was more effective than the short-term gratification of that punch. And you know what? Their ways were much more gratifying!

How do I retaliate against the wicked? Through magical curses, of course! So, let us begin the magical journey of......*SWEET REVENGE!*

THE VOCABULARY OF CURSING

These terms have specific meanings in African-American conjure:

• **Avenge:** The action of inflicting hurt or harm on someone for an injury or wrong that has been done to someone other than oneself.

• **Banish:** To force someone to leave their home town as punishment for wrongdoing and to forbid them re-entrance or return.

• **Bind:** To tie someone to a place or person; to restrain a person. In hoodoo we see the word "tie" used far more often than the word "bind."

• **Break a Curse:** To nullify or destroy a curse. Breaking a curse does not ameliorate or remediate it, nor does it return it to the one who sent it.

• **Confused in Mind:** A curse in which the victim becomes mentally muddled, cannot make decisions, and ends up shiftless or of no account.

• **Crossed Conditions:** Longstanding negative situations during which everything goes wrong; think of crossed wires in an electrical circuit.

• **Crossing, Crossed:** A non-lethal curse, worse than a jinx, less deadly than goofering; the victim is crossed up or under crossed conditions.

• **Curse:** A solemn verbal utterance intended to invoke a supernatural power to inflict harm or punishment on someone or something.

• **Evil Eye:** A sickness transmitted by an envious, jealous, or covetous person whose gaze has remained too long upon that which is coveted.

• **Fix:** To prepare or dress a magical object or tool, as with oils or powders. Also to use spiritual supplies to bring a person under control.

• **Goofer:** From Kikongo *kufwa* (to die): To lay down a powder (Goofer Dust) to cause unnatural illness, blindness, swelling, neuropathy, or death.

• **Goofer Dust:** A powder of Graveyard Dirt, reptile parts, Sulphur, Red Pepper, Black Pepper, and other items, used to goofer a victim.

• **Hex, Hexed:** From German *hexe* (witch): To cast a spell on someone, generally with bad intent; a person who is hexed is affected by witchcraft.

• **Hot Foot:** To use hot, spicy herbs and supplies to cause someone to leave a place or position abruptly and to restlessly wander the world.

• **Hurt:** A euphemism for goofering. To say, "He was hurt in his legs," indicates that the victim did not die but suffered swelling of the legs.

• **Jinx:** A person whom bad luck follows is a jinx and so is a spell that brings bad luck to others. A person who has lost his luck is said to be jinxed.

- **Jinx Killer:** A person or a spiritual supply that destroys jinxes; one may sprinkle jinx killer products on a trick laid on the ground or the floor.
- **Live Things in You:** The sensation or appearance of small living vermin crawling under your skin, up your legs, or in your abdomen.
- **Mess Them Up:** To jinx someone, run them crazy, or put them under crossed conditions; the physical supplies used are "that mess."
- **Nail Them Down:** Photos, effigies, dolls, or personal concerns are nailed or pegged in place to stop people; they can also be "tied and nailed."
- **Poison:** A euphemism that does not refer to a physical toxin but to a goofering agent that brings about an unnatural illness or death.
- **Revenge:** The act of inflicting hurt or harm on someone for an injury or wrong that one has suffered at their hands.
- **Reversing:** To return back to a person who has committed either social or spiritual evil all the work they did, in like kind and measure.
- **Run Them Crazy:** To cause mental illness, confusion in mind, aimless wandering, or irrational activities like howling or crawling on all fours.
- **Run Them Off:** To forcefully drive an unwanted person away by spiritual methods like hot footing them or whipping their tracks.
- **Throw For, Throw Roots, Root Them:** To sprinkle powders, dusts, roots, or other items to affect someone through contact magic via the feet.
- **Tie Their Nature:** To cause peoples' sexuality to be bound by controlling their libido or by completely ruining their sexual functionality.
- **Tie Their Tongues:** To stop people from talking, especially to stop verbal abuse, slander, or the giving of testimony in a court case.
- **Trick:** A magic spell; the use of contact magic to control or otherwise affect others via fixed objects without their knowledge.
- **Turn the Trick on Them:** To cleverly return a hostile worker's trick, using the same objects to affect them that he or she used to affect another.
- **Uncrossing:** To take off, wash away, ameliorate, or remediate crossed conditions. Uncrossing is not protective or restorative per se.
- **Unnatural Illness:** A physical sickness, disease, or illness whose origin is magical or the result of a curse. Doctors cannot diagnose or cure it.
- **Untie:** To get untied is to have a rootworker unmake a physical curse that had tied one's nature or one's tongue; also known as getting unwound.
- **Whip Their Tracks:** To run off an enemy by locating his footprint and repeatedly whipping it from heel to toe while cursing him by name.
- **Wither Them Away:** To cause people to slowly weaken and die.

GATHER YOUR SUPPLIES

ACQUIRE PERSONAL CONCERNS

CONCERNS OF THE BODY AND THEIR USES IN CURSING

Personal concerns are objects or items that have been connected to or associated with a person's physical body. We need this link to obtain an intimate relationship with our enemy in order to assert domination. Skin cells are the most accessible personal concerns; we shed about 30,000 to 40,000 cells an hour and regrow our epidermis once a month!

- **Hair:** Selected from various areas of the body, according to the work.
- **Fingernails and Toenails:** Related to works of the hand and to travel.
- **Sweat from the armpit:** To mark an item for a person; for body odour.
- **Menstrual Blood, fresh or dried:** For stoppage of blood, infertility.
- **Semen, fresh or dried:** For erectile dysfunction and infertility.
- **Vaginal Secretions:** For anorgasmia, vaginal odours, and infertility.
- **Urine:** In lieu of menstrual blood or semen, or for a strangury curse.
- **Feces:** For curses of constipation, bowel obstruction, insanity, and death.
- **Foot Skin Scrapings:** To cause a person to leave town and wander.
- **Skin Cells:** To mark an item for a person; for itching and skin eruptions.
- **Blood:** Very rarely used, as it is difficult to obtain; for injury or death.
- **Saliva:** To tie up the speech, to expose lies, and for loss of teeth.
- **Tears:** Rarely used, as they is difficult to obtain; for curses of sorrow.
- **Mucus:** Difficult to obtain; for nasal and lung problems and illness.
- **Ear Wax:** Difficult to obtain; can be used to bring on deafness.

ADJUNCTS TO THE BODY AND THEIR USES IN CURSING

While not pieces of the body, these traditional adjuncts have been in contact with the person or represent the person in some meaningful way:

- **Used Bath Water:** To mark an item or to gain control over a person.
- **Clothing:** To make dolls; use underwear to control or curse sexuality.
- **Dust from a Footprint:** To cause a person to leave town and wander.
- **Handwriting:** To gain for control over a person to ensure compliance.
- **Signature:** To ensure compliance with promises that were made.
- **Photograph:** To symbolize a person or to gain control over a person.

HOW TO ACQUIRE PERSONAL CONCERNS

There are many ways to collect personal concerns and it takes a clever practitioner to know just where to find them. Here are some ideas:

- **Bathroom:** Check the hairbrushes and combs for hair. Wipe down the razor, which may be loaded with hair and skin cells. Remove the sink trap and collect hair. Confiscate the waste basket and collect tissue, hair, used cotton swabs, used panty liners, or sanitary napkins. A stolen used washcloth can be cut up to make a doll.
- **Bedroom:** Use tape or a lint remover and roll it over the pillow and the sheets that have been slept on. You won't be able to see the skin cells but, you will indeed have them on the tape or lint remover. You may also encounter stray hair. Sheeting with menstrual blood or semen stains can be cut up to make packets or dolls.
- **Laundry Room:** You will want soiled, not freshly washed laundry. The hamper or washing machine may contain dirty clothes, bedding, or towels that harbour skin cells and sweat. Underwear, socks, and stained sheets are used to make cursing dolls and packets. Check the contents of the lint trap of the dryer, as hair may make its way there.
- **The Ashtray:** If your enemy is a smoker, thousands of skin cells from the lips, as well as saliva, can be found on cigarette and cigar butts. These can be used to curse the mouth, throat, and lungs.
- **While Making Love:** Tell a man that you have a fantasy of him ejaculating in your face or between your breasts, then collect the semen on a clean white cloth or a tissue. Use your fingers to masturbate a woman and then collect the vaginal secretions in the same manner.
- **Grooming Your Target:** Offering a manicure or pedicure will give you an opportunity to collect nails and cuticle skin. Tell a male target that the hair on the nape of his neck is too long and offer to clean him up. Shave with a clean dry razor and save the hair and skin.
- **Any room in the home:** Skin cells are light in weight and travel easily. In fact, most of the dust that we see is in part comprised of skin cells, so any dust that collects on furniture, equipment, window sills, or picture frames likely contains thousands of skin cells to be gathered.
- **Out of doors:** If only cement paths are to be found near the home or place of business, lightly sprinkling dirt where the person will walk will allow you to collect foot-track dirt. Scrape it up with a spatula.

SELECT TRADITIONAL CURSING PRODUCTS

DRESSING AND ANOINTING OILS FOR CURSING

Many people wonder why we dress our tools with oils. The answer is simple: they possess the magical properties of herbs, roots, and minerals. Why are these ingredients magical? Because the aforementioned elements are spiritual entities, and these spirits, even after death, can assist us, just as if we had called upon the spirit of a deceased human for help.

Top quality oils contain one or more natural components possessing the magical aspects that assist with and enhance the desired results of our spells. When performing curses of revenge, it is imperative to have all the spiritual help that we can get.

- **Banishing Oil:** To remove unwanted people or conditions.
- **Bat's Blood Oil:** For enemy work.
- **Black Arts Oil:** A powerful aid in destruction spells.
- **Break Up Oil:** To cause people to fight, separate, and divorce.
- **Confusion Oil:** To cause confusion and befuddlement.
- **Crossing Oil:** To trick, cross, and mess up the life of an enemy.
- **Damnation Oil:** To curse a wrong-doer to suffer in Hell.
- **Destruction Oil:** For the destruction of enemies.
- **Devil's Oil:** To harm or cause mischief to others.
- **Double Cross Oil:** To dress innocent-seeming gifts to harm another.
- **D.U.M.E. Oil:** Death Unto My Enemies — self-explanatory.
- **Hot Foot Oil:** To physically drive someone away.
- **Inflammatory Confusion Oil:** For misunderstandings and fights.
- **Jinx Oil:** To puts jinxes, bad luck, and trouble on others.
- **Restless Oil:** To cause turmoil, loss of sleep, and mental disturbances.
- **Revenge Oil:** To exact harsh justice on a wrong-doer.
- **Reversing Oil:** To send back all evil that an enemy sent to you.

Among rootworkers, these oils are known as conjure oils, hoodoo oils, dressing oils, condition oils, prepared oils, ritual oils, or anointing oils. Their names usually describe the condition they are intended to cause or cure. All of them are appropriate for cursing, crossing, or jinxing work:

For further instructions on the use of oils in hoodoo, see this web page: **LuckyMojo.com/oils.html by Catherine Yronwode**

MINERAL DUSTS AND SACHET POWDERS FOR CURSING

Mineral dusts, powdered herbs and roots, and compounded sachet powders have a special role in hoodoo because they derive from ancient African foot-track magic that has been preserved to the present day. Powders containing single or compounded minerals and herbs are the oldest form of dusts used in spells of cursing and revenge.

- **Black Pepper Powder:** To drive off evil and protect from sorcery.
- **Goofer Dust:** To weaken or kill an enemy through contact magic.
- **Graveyard Dirt:** To put a particular graveyard spirit on an enemy.
- **Red Pepper Powder:** To hot foot people and send them wandering.
- **Sulphur Powder:** To send someone to the realm of Fire and Brimstone.

Spiritual sachet powders have the same condition names and herbal ingredients as their allied dressing oils on page 12, and may be thought of as "condition powders." They are deployed by sprinkling and dusting.
For more information on the use of sachet powders in hoodoo see:
LuckyMojo.com/powders.html by Catherine Yronwode

BATH HERBS, SALTS, AND FLOOR WASHES FOR CURSING

Mineral salts, bath crystals, and floor washes are used in contact magic.

- **Alum Crystals:** To shut an enemy's mouth, urethra, or genital organs.
- **Boric Acid:** Used as a spreading agent for herbs in foot-track magic.
- **Epsom Salts:** Mixed with Graveyard Dirt to disarm an enemy.
- **Salt:** Salt, useful for so many things, can also be used to hurt an enemy.
- **Saltpeter:** To cause impotence or to drag someone down.
- **Vinegar:** To sour someone's life or to sour a relationship.
- **War Water:** To declare war, bring on a conflict, or move someone out.

Mineral bath salts or "condition baths" have the same names and herbal ingredients as the dressing oils on page 12. To use them, dissolve a 2 oz. packet into 64 ounces of warm water and pour the liquid into four 16 oz. bottles. Put it into spray bottles to spritz property or belongings, freeze it for future use or to make freezer spells, or add it to an enemy's laundry water.
For more information on bath crystals see this web page:
LuckyMojo.com/bath.html by Catherine Yronwode

INCENSES FOR CURSING

Incenses have been used in ritual practices since the ancient times. Even the Bible tell us to use incense, for in Exodus 30:01 it is said: *"Thou shalt make an altar to burn incense on"* and in 2 Chronicles 13:11 we find that *"... they burn unto the Lord every morning and every evening burnt sacrifices and sweet incense ..."*

Incense can carry messages directly to our targets or to the Spirit world. Some practitioners believe that because Spirits are attracted to the smoke and odour of incense, it is easier to summon and ask for their assistance by using incense. This is why we pray, state our petition, or scream our curses while the incense is burning.

Incense comes in a number of different forms such as:

- **Natural Resins:** The hardened sap of trees; burned on charcoal.
- **Wood Chips:** Burned on charcoal alone or with herbs or resins.
- **Herbs:** Burned on charcoal, either with other herbs or with resins.
- **Agarbatti or Joss Sticks:** Convenient and quick-burning.
- **Cones and Logs:** Self-lighting and long-burning.
- **Coils:** They need a special holder but are very long-burning.
- **Powders:** May be mixed with herbs or resins; often self-lighting.

Loose powder incenses have the same condition names as the oils on page 12, making them "condition incenses." Just as with sachet powders and bath crystals, they are compounded to achieve certain desired effects.

Powder incenses can also be used in ways other than burning. For example, they can be used in lieu of sachet powders when laying tricks. I also personally love to roll my anointed candles in powder incense because it achieves a dual effect: First, the candle flame pierces the veil between our world and the Spirit World and makes it easier for us to contact the entities. Secondly, while the candle flame is actively ablaze, it will also continuously summon the Spirits as it burns the incense!

In the 1936 book *Legends of Incense, Herb, and Oil Magic* by Lewis de Claremont, we are told that we can make our own condition incense simply by adding the desired condition oils and the appropriate powdered herbs into a high quality self-lighting black incense powder.

For further information about incenses see this web page:
LuckyMojo.com/incense.html by Catherine Yronwode

HERBS AND ROOTS FOR CURSING

In my personal opinion, the very best and most comprehensive presentation of the purpose and usage of herbs, minerals, animal curios, in Hoodoo is the book *Hoodoo Herb and Root Magic* by Catherine Yronwode. It is so valuable to thousands of conjure practitioners that many of us affectionately refer to it as "The Green Bible." Therefore, it will be our reference formulary for the use of natural herbs, roots, minerals, and zoological curios in cursing magic:

- **Aloes Powder (Bitter Aloes):** Used in graveyard bottle spells to silence the lips of those who speak evil.
- **Asafoetida (Devil's Dung):** To jinx or get revenge on an enemy.
- **Bittersweet (Climbing Bittersweet):** To cross an enemy's path.
- **Black (Brown) Mustard Seed:** Causes confusion and despair.
- **Black Pepper:** For a hurtful bottle spell or a revenge candle spell.
- **Black Snake Root (Black Cohosh, Bugbane):** To move unwanted people out of your home.
- **Black Walnut Leaves:** To kill an enemy's luck.
- **Blueberry:** To bring sorrow to an enemy.
- **Cactus:** Natural pins and needles with which to stab doll-babies.
- **Celandine:** Causes confusion and wandering mind.
- **Chicory:** To strengthen a curse.
- **Chia Seed:** To stop gossip and shut people up.
- **Couch Grass (Witch's Grass, Dog Grass, Quack Grass, Twitch Grass, Quitch Grass):** To trouble enemies with nerve complaints.
- **Cruel (or Old) Man of the Woods:** Secreted on the enemy to hurt.
- **Dogbane (Bitter Root):** A jinxing and crossing herb.
- **Grains of Paradise:** Can be used for jinxing (and also for blessings).
- **Jezebel Root:** Used for a specific curse called "The Curse of Jezebel."
- **Poppy Seeds:** Causes confusion and forgetfulness of the mind.
- **Red Pepper:** Causes anger and break-ups; makes people move.
- **Skunk Cabbage (Pole Cat Weed):** Crosses and jinxes' enemies.
- **Snake Head (Balmony):** To cause an enemy to get sick.
- **Spanish Moss:** A powerful jinxing material for evil work.
- **Sweet Gum:** To cause an enemy pain or get them out of your life.
- **Tobacco:** Can be used as a jinxing incense.
- **Vandal Root (Valerian):** To jinx an enemy or stop unwanted visitors.

ANIMAL CURIOS FOR CURSING

Although all forms of worldwide folk magic have included spells in which animals are tortured, the majority of contemporary practitioners believe that all animals, even those called "vermin," have a right to live a normal life. There are enough cursing spells that make use of deceased animals or remnant concerns that we do not need to become animal abusers in order to do magical harm. Most of the zoological curios listed here can be found or purchased in the form of dead animals. Others can be acquired at pet stores or from friends and neighbours who keep pets.

- **Ants (Horse Ants, Fire Ants, Red Ants, Crazy Ants):** To force an enemy to wander; to run a woman crazy; to cause urinary problems.
- **Bat and Bullbat (Whippoorwill):** Used in death spells.
- **Black Hen's Eggs:** Used with other ingredients to harm an enemy.
- **Cockroaches:** Dead Roaches accompany placed dolls in coffins.
- **Cowrie Shell:** They look like female genitals, thus they are used for cursing female genitalia.
- **Dirt Dauber Nest:** Destroys enemies; causes confusion.
- **Dog Feces:** To cause your enemy to be looked at in disgust.
- **Flies and Maggots:** To cause disgust, confusion, filth, and disease.
- **Frogs**: Eating Frog spawn causes "live things" in you.
- **Ground Puppies (Ground Dogs, Mud Puppies):** For "live things."
- **Horse Hair:** Horses are neutral, but those who drink trough-water and swallow a Horse hair develop "live things" in them.
- **Lizards:** Used the same way that Snakes are used.
- **Rats:** A dead Rat may accompany a doll that represents a thief or liar into its coffin for burial in a graveyard.
- **Scorpions:** Dead Scorpions are laid in coffins with dolls to be buried.
- **Snails:** Dried Snails stop people, especially women, from having sex.
- **Snakes:** The blood, eggs, flesh, bones, sheds, and skins of Snakes, especially poisonous species like Rattlesnake, Copperhead, and Cottonmouth, are for jinxing and crossing or to cause "live things."
- **Spiders:** Eating Spider eggs causes "live things" in you; Tarantula exoskeletons make impressively horrific coverings for enemy dolls.

Find further information on herbs, minerals and animal curios at: **LuckyMojo.com/mojocatherbs.html**

Cursing products offered in hoodoo mail order catalogues, 1935 - 2017. Art by Charles M. Quinlan, Charles C. Dawson, K. Rudin, charlie wiley, Jean-Baptiste Alliette, Oswald Wirth, nagasiva yronwode, and catherine yronwode for Oracle, Valmor Products, and Lucky Mojo.

WORK WITH NAMES AND PETITION PAPERS

Not all spells employ written papers, but every worker should know how to make them. There are two types, name papers and petition papers.

A name paper is a slip of paper with the name and possibly the birth date of a person. It is a less-than-personal form of personal concern.

A petition is simply a written spell. It can contain a request, a wish, a command, a prayer from scripture, or glyphs, as you choose.

We often write petitions on name papers, so the papers do double-duty.

To make a basic cursing petition, tear a square piece of brown grocery bag that does not contain any factory folds, designs, letterings, or cuts. Write out the enemy's name 9 or 13 times, once on each line, each line directly below the other. Turn the paper 90 degrees and write a command over the names 9 or 13 times in the same fashion. (9 and 13 are not required numbers; they are examples.)

Usually, my command is one word that correlates with the products I am using. For example, if I am using Destruction products, my command is *Destruction*. If I have chosen D.U.M.E. products, my command is *Death*. Other people write their commands in full sentences. The choice is yours.

Next I anoint the petition paper with my cursing oil in a "5-Spot" pattern — a dot of oil at the upper left corner, the upper right corner, the lower right corner, the lower left corner, and, finally, a dot in the middle.

Finally I fold a cursing paper once away from myself, turn the paper to the left, and fold it again away from myself. There are other ways to fold a paper; this is probably the simplest method.

Lastly, I find that it if I am undertaking a lengthy series of curses against one person, it is convenient for me to make several of these petitions papers in one sitting and enclose them in an air-tight storage container. That way, they are easily accessible and available.

When performing candle work, these papers can be placed under the candle holder or directly under the candle. If working with large, thick candles, the candle may be partially hollowed out and the paper may be placed within it. This is called loading the candle. Personal concerns and herbal curios may be loaded into the candle at the same time as the paper.

When working with container spells such as mirror boxes, freezer spells, flower pots, and bottle or jar spells, the papers usually go inside the containers. They may also be hidden inside hand-sewn doll-babies.

PETITIONS ON OTHER MEDIA

In her book *Paper in My Shoe,* Catherine Yronwode notes that names and petitions can be written on many surfaces other than paper:

- **Candle Wax:** Use a needle, pin, nail, or thorn to inscribe names and commands on free-standing candles. It is traditional to do this in the form of spirals, like the stripes on a barber pole.
- **White China Plates:** Ink, menstrual blood, beet juice, or other coloured fluids are used to write on the plate, then washed off for use in cooking, bathing, or other forms of spell preparation.
- **Money:** Used in the preparation of spells involving wealth or the destruction of an enemy's wealth.
- **Signed Checks:** A form of personal concern, since they are signed.
- **Company Logos:** For job-getting or to curse a business in some way.
- **Eggs:** To curse people or move them out, eggs are often written on all over, with the enemy's name in helter-skelter and random fashion.
- **Aluminum Foil:** When fixing an animal-tongue freezer curse, write your curse with a ball-point pen on the foil in which you wrap it.
- **Aluminum Pie Plates and Tea Light Cups:** Inscribed in the same way that aluminum foil is, these are fire-safe bases for candle work.
- **Popsicle Sticks:** Used in binding spells; the people eat the popsicles, then the sticks are named and tied together, name side in.
- **Seals:** It is a very old-fashioned trick to write one's command over an appropriate seal or symbol from *The Key of Solomon, The Sixth and Seventh Books of Moses,* or *The Black Pullet.*
- **Business Cards:** To mess up a man's finances, write a curse on his business card, dress it with cursing oil, and burn it, saying, *"As this card is consumed in flame, so is John Doe and [the name of his company]."*
- **Photographs:** A paper print of the enemy's photo can be dressed and glued to a vigil candle as a label or folded into a packet around a pinch of cursing powders or harsh herbs for burial or for burning.
- **Playing and Tarot Cards:** Cards can be written on, then burned buried, hidden, or used in lieu of a petition paper. Additionally, their images can be printed out and made into labels for vigil candles.

For more information on written spells, papers, and petitions, read: **"Paper In My Shoe" by Catherine Yronwode**

ASSEMBLE THE TOOLS OF TORTURE

Because cursing can produce physical as well as mental effects, it is traditional to use physical items to cause pain and grief to the effigies of our enemies. Here are some traditional tools used to torment effigies or to include in bottle, jar, or coffin spells.

- **Barbeque Grill:** Clay or dough dolls can be grilled to cause severe pain to the enemy. Wax dolls can be melted away to death.
- **Baseball Bat:** Used to beat and soften up a pliable cloth doll.
- **Boards:** Boards or heavy sticks can also be used to beat dolls.
- **Broken Glass:** Most commonly found in container spells, shards of broken glass can also be used to inflict pain to most effigies.
- **Coffin Nails:** Nails that have been removed from a coffin, were found in a graveyard, or have been kept in Graveyard Dirt can cause death by transferring the illness of the deceased person to the enemy.
- **Drill:** Used to bore holes into figural candles for ease of loading personal concerns, herbs, and petitions; to cause pain to an enemy; or to bore a hole into a tree to plug an enemy's sex or bowels up.
- **Duct Tape:** Used for binding an effigy.
- **Freezer:** Effigies of rivals and enemies who are to be placed "on ice" or "frozen out" of situations are set in the back of a freezer.
- **Frying Pan:** Use a cast iron skillet to fry names, photos, and dolls; it is also a fire-safe container in which to burn alcoholic perfumes.
- **Hammer:** Used to smash a wax, twig, or clay effigy to pieces.
- **Ice Pick:** To cause pain to specific body areas by jabbing the effigy.
- **Knife:** For torment by stabbing or cutting the enemy's effigy.
- **Lighter or Matches:** Obviously, fire hurts! Used to cause pain by repeated edge-singeing or to devour the effigy in fire.
- **Metal Shavings:** Sharp, tiny metal shards can be used in container spells to inflict ongoing generalized pain.
- **Mirrors:** For reversing spells that reflect evil back to the evil-doer; also, broken mirror pieces in container spells cause bad luck and pain.
- **Moth Balls:** These contain poisons. Use them carefully to stuff a doll's mouth or even to stuff the entire body of a doll.
- **Mould:** Used for stuffing dolls or to place on effigies to cause yeast infections and allergies; also used inside wax goofer balls.

- **Nails or Tacks:** Rusty nails are used to prick effigies or are placed in container spells that will be shaken up to cause pain, illnesses, or death.
- **Needles:** Can be used for carving names on candles. As with nails, they are used to prick effigies and are ingredients in bottle spells.
- **Pins:** As with nails, tacks, and needles, pins are used to prick the effigies and are a part of damaging bottle spells that are shaken.
- **Rat Poison Pellets:** Used for stuffing effigies to poison the enemy with severe illness or death.
- **Razor Blades:** For container spells and to inflict pain on or to slice and cut an effigy.
- **Rocks:** Large rocks can be used just as a hammer to smash an effigy to pieces.
- **Rope:** Used for binding effigies. Also, used to tie nooses around an effigy's neck and hung out on a tree branch or other high places to prepare for beatings.
- **Rust:** Just as the nature of rust stains and deteriorates metal so to it stains or deteriorates the enemy. Can either be used for stuffing a poppet or placed in container spells.
- **Saw:** A small handsaw can be used for amputation of an effigy.
- **Skunk Gland Essence:** Used in container spells or poured on effigies which are then bottled up to cause the enemy to be disgusting to anyone who approaches. Wear gloves, because skunk essence stinks to high heaven and the odour is difficult to eradicate.
- **Soldering Iron:** As with the drill, used to either bore holes into figural candles (for loading with ingredients and/or petitions) or simply to cause pain to the enemy.
- **Staple Gun:** To inflict pain and torment to a construction worker.
- **Stapler:** To inflict pain and torment to an office worker.
- **String or Thread:** To bind, tie down, or strangulate the effigy.
- **Toxic Medications:** "Fed" into a doll to produce an overdose.
- **War Water:** Used for laying tricks by poisoning the feet. Also, causes conflict and tension. Can also be used in container spells.
- **Whip:** A horse whip or cat-o-nine-tails can be used to whip someone's foot-tracks or to punish a doll-baby.
- **Wires:** Used for binding or strangling effigies.
- **Vinegar:** Used for cursing enemies and to sour their lives. Most commonly used n container or freezer spells.

PREPARE YOUR MIND AND SOUL

ASK YOURSELF: IS THIS CURSE JUSTIFIED?

Curses inflicted on someone out of jealousy, bias, prejudice, or paranoia are simply aggressive. They rarely can be said to have the power of divine justice behind them. So, although there are many forms of cursing in folk magic, only curses of revenge are held by most people to be justified.

What is revenge? It is a basic instinct that we all possess, defined as "the act of inflicting hurt or harm on someone for an injury or wrong that one has suffered at their hands."

In everyday life, most of us encounter folks who have no respect, regard, or consideration for others. They have no boundaries. They invade our personal spaces while disrupting our sense of self-preservation. They are just downright rude and nasty!

Do we want revenge for how they treated us? Of course, we do! And we seek that revenge in our thoughts, words, and our actions. But ought we go as far as to perform magical curses on every single rude or nasty person who crosses our path?

I deal with vulgar people on a daily basis. There are many times that I think to myself: "You think you're so tough? Well, I'll get you!" But I also know that magical cursing is a serious matter. So I wait about a week and reassess my feelings toward the person who upset me. Sometimes I will have forgotten about the rude deed they did. More often my natural good temper will have reasserted itself and my anger will have subsided. In either case, I will be grateful that I didn't waste my time, energy, or money on supplies for cursing that idiot asshole!

When we are extremely angry and perform cursing spells without clear thought, we can do serious harm and the spells can go beyond our initial intentions. Cursing a man in the heat of the moment may indeed result in his death, but what about his orphaned child, who will now grow up without a dad and become a career criminal? That's not what we intended.

The Bible states in Exodus 21:24, *"Eye for eye, tooth for tooth, hand for hand, foot for foot..."* In other words, the punishment must be commensurate with the crime. So, before you curse, calm down and think about the entire situation. "Revenge," as the saying goes, "is a dish best served cold."

CREATE A PLAN OF ACTION

THE POWER OF CUMULATIVE SPELL EFFECTS

While it is true that a hastily-flung "double whammy" has tripped up and brought low many a foe, we cannot count on always being able to catch a powerful enemy off-guard. After all, the truly evil ones know that they are doing wrong and have hardened themselves against retaliation.

Begin with a curse that is centered on a single method, such as prayer or foot-track magic, or has one basic ingredient, such as a Lemon, Goofer Dust, or War Water. If your enemy is unguarded, weak, unjustified in God's eyes, or has no allies in his spiritual court, you may be able to upend him quickly. One spell may be all it takes to kill a man, if it is God's holy will.

If you see no omens of success after three days, watch and wait for three weeks to determine if the situation is shows movement toward your goal. If not, add a second simple job of a different type, perhaps a candle spell, or a freezer spell this time. After another three weeks, if no progress has been made, add a third spell, perhaps a more complex one.

In this way you can test the target's vulnerability. A brief contact spell may achieve your goal, but even if it does not, it will cause a negative effect. Remaining persistent despite lack of movement, you will continue to load cumulative negative energies into his life, planning to eventually burden him down with the proverbial straw that breaks the Camel's back.

If three months go by and no change has occurred, you can be sure that either your foe is shielded by ancestors, evil spirits, or a clever application of his own conjure knowledge, or that God has decided, for reasons unknown, to deny your petition. You will not anger God if you ask again. In fact, you may now move to a more complex form of spell if needed.

HOW LONG WILL IT TAKE?

Professional rootworkers find this question difficult to answer. I know of a case in which a single pink crucifix candle and a sincere prayer brought about the justified murder of a career criminal. I also know that my own grandmother beat an effigy doll daily for a year before her enemy's life began to come apart and his reputation withered away.

Remember, too, that God has the final say. If the man whom you are cursing is slated by God to be "The Hero of the Hotel Fire" two years from now, you will not be able to kill him until his work on Earth is done.

BEGIN THE WORK BY CLEANSING YOURSELF

Once you have decided that a curse is justified, or that you wish to perform it regardless, you should enter into the work clean in body and mind. Let me ask you exactly what I ask my clients when they are seeking personal magical coaching from me: "If you haven't taken a bath for a year, and then donned perfume, how will you smell?"

The answer is that you will still smell bad. I compare this sad state of affairs to those who try to practice rootwork when they're not spiritually clean. Negative vibrations have latched onto them. Their work will stink.

How do we pick up spiritual "dirt"? Well, every day, most of us encounter crazy energies. In addition to the grumbling of busy people under stress, we also encounter people who are angry, mentally unstable, or of impure heart.

Almost every time that I am in my car, someone either annoys or infuriates me. Or perhaps, because of my cautious driving, I annoy or infuriate them. What happens? We may exchange nasty words or gestures, but more often we intentionally or unintentionally deliver the evil eye, mutter imprecations, and exchange jinxes until the air around us is filled with bad vibrations.

Then there are the dramatists who misuse our time. These are the folks who tell us all their problems under the guise of asking for advice which they will never take. The worst of them are actually psychic vampires who drain others of strength and power in order to replenish their own energies.

After a day of this, we return home either depleted of energy or with bad vibrations attached to us. In other words, we are in a weakened state because we are spiritually dirty — and it is very difficult to effectively implement and execute spells of any kind while in such a fragile spiritual position.

For these reasons, almost all the root doctors I know begin every job of work with a bath. There are many traditional recipes for these baths, from Van Van and Chinese Wash to Kosher Salt scrubs and Uncrossing Crystals, but the mixture known as 13 Herb Bath is my preference. It removes jinxes and takes off crossed conditions, and it is also refreshing and rejuvenating.

Read more about spiritual baths and floor washes on this web page:
LuckyMojo.com/baths.html
Further details on 13 Herb Bath can be found online here:
Herb-magic.com/13herb-bath-one-html
This entire book is devoted to authentic recipes and spells for cleansing:
"Hoodoo Spiritual Baths" by Aura Laforest

PROTECT YOURSELF AND YOUR FAMILY

Anoint yourself with protection once you step out of your bath. You are spiritually clean and will attract negativity just as white clothing will attract dirt. A spiritual overcoat will protect your from becoming "dirty" again.

Bathing is recommended before any kind of conjure work, but cursing, by its nature, entails the risk of certain dangers. The most common are not thinking a spell through and doing it wrong, attracting malevolent spirits who are drawn to negative energy, or working so sloppily that the enemy becomes aware of our work and reverses or turns the trick back on us. It is absolutely necessary to protect ourselves from these unwanted outcomes.

My usual routine when cursing is this: After I have cleansed the house with Chinese Wash and sprayed the rooms with Florida Water, I take my spiritual bath. Immediately after the bath, I anoint myself with Fiery Wall of Protection Oil. The anointing process starts at the base of my spine and proceeds all the way up my back to my neck and the crown of my head. Then I anoint my front side, starting with my solar plexus, to my heart, and finally, to my throat. I also wear protection amulets as I work.

Fiery Wall of Protection Oil, Protection Oil, Archangel Michæl Oil, or Guardian Angel Oil are good and traditional spiritual supplies for personal protection. Some people prefer to dust their bodies with a sachet powder rather than apply an oil, and that is equally traditional. The choice is yours.

After protecting yourself, it is your duty to protect the beings who live with you from being caught up in your cursing work. You will be creating harmful energies aimed toward your enemy, and negative spells that are not sent out with a distinct recipient in mind can attach themselves to family members, pets, or other creatures who get in the way and are not protected.

Several times I have unexpectedly found dead insects in and around my working space during or after performing curses. Unfortunately, they were vulnerable and in the "line of fire." Therefore, one of my essential rules is that, for safety's sake, I do not allow pets, children, or adults near my cursing work. This not only ensures my privacy, it also ensures their well-being.

A traditional way to limit the "collateral damage" you might do and at the same time increase the power of your work is to keep your mind focussed and to clearly call the name of the one whom you are working against. If your curse includes recital from scripture, the text should be altered to include his name. This is known as "quoting him in."

REALIZE YOUR STRENGTH AND POWER

We have prepared ourselves emotionally to curse. We have calmed down, thought about the situation, and determined that we are justified to seek revenge. We have bathed and dressed ourselves with protection, and taken steps to see to the safety of our family, pets, and friends.

Now it is time to work on our attitude, to prime ourselves, both in mind and body, to wield power and dominion. We will develop and maintain:

- **Self-Confidence:** To know we are strong enough to control the enemy.
- **Patience:** To observe results and work within a time-frame.
- **Persistence:** To repeat a spell or try a different one as needed.
- **Determination:** To see the work through to its ultimate conclusion.
- **Strength of Will:** To maintain our resolve against opposing forces.
- **Faith:** To recognize God as the final arbiter and judge of all.

Always remember that we must be in complete control of the situation. Whatever we want to happen to our enemies WILL happen. Our foes are to become our victims, our prisoners, our puppets. We are the masters, while the objects of our attacks are nothing but useless, insignificant pieces of garbage. Faced with our knowledge, our wills, our perseverance, and the spiritual court of energies which will assist us, our enemies are helpless.

Some spiritual supply products that address these issues are:

- **Commanding:** For leadership, to rally spiritual forces to your side.
- **Compelling:** To force someone to act in a certain way, against his will.
- **Controlling:** To take over the mind and actions of another.
- **Do as I Say:** To enhance commanding verbal power over another.
- **Domination:** To utterly cow and rule another through force of will.
- **Essence of Bend-Over:** To cause a person to accede to your desires.
- **I Can You Can't:** To gain the victory when only one person can win.
- **Master:** To exemplify authority, rulership, command, and courage.

Apply powder or anoint yourself with one or more of these oils in an upward motion, I usually anoint my hands, arms, shoulders, the area around my lips (so that my words have power) and, finally, my third eye (the area between the eyebrows, the gate of higher consciousness).

PREPARE YOUR WORK SPACE

PROTECT THE AREA AROUND YOU

Catherine Yronwode teaches four basic ways to protect your working space: "Shield yourself through spiritual invisibility, attract good spirits to shield you, set up 'cross-me-not' barriers, and repel evil generally."

Shielding your room through invisibility can be as simple as laying out four Bay leaves in the corners. You can also dust your hands with Agar Agar powder, or sprinkle it on your table top before laying down an altar cloth. Additionally, mirrors that face outward deflect attention from your work.

Attracting good spirits depends in part upon our beliefs. For some of us, the Archangel Michæl, the Lord God of Hosts, or the Blood of Jesus provide heavenly shielding. For others, the Ancestors are the primary guardians.

A barrier shield prevents anything untoward from entering your home. Think of it as a massive steel wall around your house — but before you build that wall, be sure not to lock in any negative energies. Clutter is a hiding place for spiritual messes. Before erecting a barrier, free your work space from clutter and ensure that nearby areas are clean. Chinese Wash will help tremendously. Follow up by spritzing the air with Florida Water.

Place barriers at doorways and windows. I use amulets in these places, but other workers prefer Bat Nuts, Camphor squares and dimes, or herb packets. At all entrance doors, I keep a votive cup of Florida Water, and I may add Camphor to the liquid. Professor Charles Porterfield tells me that down in Texas, folks use Vicks VapoRub to 5-spot the doors and windows, because the Camphor and Eucalyptus in it repel bad spirits, and some folks use Ammonia or Turpentine to repel the "undesirables." I draw lines with Fiery Wall of Protection Oil at all window sills and thresholds. Some people draw lines with Salt or Red Brick Dust, as these too are protective.

To repel evil, I have a Bible opened to Psalms 121 beneath my bed. Over this page is an opened pair of scissors, pointing to the head of the Bible. Alongside this, there is another votive cup of Florida Water with Camphor.

For an array of other protection tactics see this page online:

LuckyMojo.com/protectionspells.html

For more on Chinese Wash and Florida Water see:

LuckyMojo.com/chinesewash.html
LuckyMojo.com/floridakanangawater.html

SET UP YOUR ALTAR

For some reason, the topic of altars frequently confuses and intimidates newcomers to the practice of magic. This is because some altars are elaborate and ornate and because many books and web sites demand that all practitioners must establish and maintain a rigid and complicated set-up. The bottom line in hoodoo and other forms of folk magic is that complication is not necessary.

Hoodoo developed among slaves and impoverished people. Did all of them have the resources, time, or privacy for fancy altars? Absolutely not! They made do with what they had and their spells nevertheless worked. Yes, professional spiritual workers, especially after Emancipation and during the 20th century, have often built altars, but the daily practitioner might just as easily work on the floor, in the old African way, or on a convenient table, with or without a black or white cloth covering. An altar is simply a space for a religious or spiritual ritual. We can make them ornate or plain, temporary or permanent, as we desire.

To some folks, East represents the new beginnings of sunrise, South symbolizes the abundance of noon, West signifies the removals of sunset, and North stands for the darkness of death. They face their altars according to the planned outcome of their work, so curses face West or North.

To others, East represents air; South represents fire; West represents water; and North represents earth, so they place tools on their altars in accordance with the corresponding directions — incense at the East, candles at the South, liquids at the West, and herbs or minerals at the North.

As for where to place an altar for cursing, I advocate only a few rules:

For safety reasons I do not recommend placing a cursing altar where you, your family, friends, or pets regularly relax, eat, or sleep.

I do not recommend working negative magic concurrently with positive magic such as prosperity, love, healing, or success spells on the same altar. In fact, many spiritual practitioners, including myself, maintain distinctly separate areas for different types of work. In other words, we use one room, or one side of a room, for negative magical spells and another room, or another side of the room, for positive magical spells. In the summertime, I prefer working my negative magical spells outdoors.

For more information on hoodoo altars and their placement read:

"Hoodoo Shrines and Altars" by Miss Phoenix LeFæ

IDEAS FOR INDOOR ALTARS
Indoor altars need not be dedicated spaces; set them up as needed.

- **Table or Work Bench:** Used coffee tables, kitchen tables, side tables and carpenters' work benches can be found at thrift stores.
- **Bureau:** The top of a bedroom bureau, chest of drawers, chifforobe, dresser, or makeup table makes a good private altar in one's bedroom.
- **Desk:** Sneaky tricks can be placed underneath or in a drawer.
- **Kitchen Cabinet:** An upper kitchen cabinet is a good place to store hidden materials and ongoing spells that we'll add to food.
- **Closet Shelf:** The upper shelf in a closet is a good place to build an altar that you need to keep hidden or secret.
- **Behind the Commode:** This is the perfect place to keep cursing or break-up spells; it is also a traditional place to store vinegar jar spells.
- **Woodshed, Tool-shed, or Garage:** Cursing work can be kept away from the house but still conducted indoors if you have outbuildings.

IDEAS FOR OUTDOOR ALTARS
Outdoor work spaces often do double-duty as garden features.

- **Patio:** A patio can be used for almost any type of altar, especially if it is screened in and safe from the weather. Try outfitting a portable buffet table, console cabinet, wooden keg, or wine barrel as an altar.
- **Barbeque Pit:** A barbeque pit is fire-safe for burning candles. You can also use it for cursing, to put heat to someone, or to leave a doll-baby in a dark sooty place or to combust the doll-baby.
- **Garden:** Build an altar in your own garden. Rock or brick elements will stand up to the elements when not in use.
- **Trees:** You can send forth desires into the world by placing them among the leaves of trees, hide things in hollow tress, and stop an enemy's life force by pegging it into a hole drilled into a tree.
- **Crossroads:** A crossroads is a place where rootworkers may leave spell remains, but it can also be used as an altar.
- **Graveyard:** A graveyard altar or bench may be used as a temporary altar. Also, consider taking problems to the gravesite and burying them there. Additionally, you can build a makeshift cemetery in our own back yard, or at you enemy's doorstep.

LAY TRICKS AND DISPOSE OF THE REMAINS

A trick is a magical spell. To lay down a trick is to deploy it at or under the ground where the victim with contact it with his shoes or feet. Tricked items can also be deployed by other forms of contact, such as touching the victim's body or clothes, oiling doorknobs, or serving tricked food or drink. The mechanism by which the victim is affected is called "contagious magic" by anthropologists and "contact work" by root doctors.

DEPLOYMENT ON PATHS, PORCHES, AND FLOORS

This is the classic hoodoo method — to sprinkle or bury cursing items such as a powder, roots, herbs, an egg, or a bottle so your victim will step on, over, or beside them and be affected. Tricks of this type are among the oldest methods, and the only difficulty they poses in modern times is that you must beware of security cameras.

Powders are usually laid down inconspicuously, so that the victim will not notice them. Experienced workers mix powders with local soil to reduce their visibility. Some like to blow powders off the palm of the hand to barely coat surfaces with dust; others work the powders into carpeting.

DEPLOYMENT IN CLOTHING AND FABRIC

Try not to use cursing oils on fabric. They will be noticeable, and as a result, people will just wash or wipe them off. Instead, trick fabric by smoking it with incense, washing it with a prepared bath salts, or spritzing it with an herb tea or with bath crystals dissolved in water.

- **Inside Socks and Shoes:** A modified form of foot-track work.
- **Inside Hats and Headbands:** To affect the victim's mind.
- **Inside Gloves:** To cripple the hands with arthritis.
- **Inside the Pants Legs:** To hobble motion or cause pain in the legs.
- **Inside the Arms of Shirts:** To bring about weakness of the limbs.
- **Inside Pockets:** To cause loss of money and luck.
- **Inside Pillow Cases:** For nightmares, sleep apnea, and death.
- **Under the Sheets or Mattress:** For body aches and pains.

Read more about laying tricks and disposing of ritual remains here:
LuckyMojo.com/layingtricks.html by Catherine Yronwode

THE SPELLS

CURSING THE BODY

COFFIN NAILS AND CLOTHING NAILED TO A TREE
This is an old hoodoo curse from the area around Wilmington, North Carolina. It is also known in Savannah, Georgia. During the 1930s, quite a few practitioners told variations of it to Harry Hyatt. This is my version.

Get an article of clothing from your victim. The closer it was worn to the skin, the better; an undershirt is better than a jacket, and the seat of the underpants is better yet. Take the clothing, a hammer, and nine coffin nails to a far-away and sturdy tree that is not visible to people. It should not be in a deep forest, because we want the Sun to strike its trunk, but it should be outside of town, because we don't want anyone to take our curse down. On the sunny side of that tree, from the East, through the South, and on to the West, is where the article of clothing will be nailed.

Spread out the clothing to ensure that it is entirely exposed to the sun. Hammer nine coffin nails through and into the tree. With each strike of the hammer, scream the target's name and the curse out loud. When you have finished, walk away and do not return to that tree.

Your victim will become weaker and weaker with each changing Moon phase. He will be nailed down and run crazy. There also ought to be signs of withering away from dehydration as the clothing fades from exposure to sunlight. Next spring, "When the sap goes up, he will go down."

URINE IN THE FIREPLACE FOR BLADDER TROUBLES
All along the East Coast, from New York City through Albermarle, Virginia; Wilson, North Carolina; Brunswick, Georgia; and down to Saint Petersburg, Florida, Harry Hyatt met workers who told him a very old curse that consists of throwing your victim's urine into a fireplace. Some said it would run you crazy, others said it would give you urinary problems, and a few said that if it was done right, it would kill you.

Most folks told Hyatt to just to throw the urine loose into the flames, but a few said to confine it in a bottle. Mrs. Baker, born in Albermarle, told it this way, "They get some of your water in a bottle and cork it up, dig a hole in the corner of the chimney and bury this upside down; and when this water would boil, you die."

DR. JOHANNES' CONSTIPATION AND DIARRHEA SPELL

You need something cylindrical from your enemy. A straw from a drink, a bottleneck from their beer, a ring, or even a rolled-up business card will do. This cylinder will be their intestines and you will name it as such.

If possible, get a piece of their underwear and cut out the piece where their ass has been. The cut-out piece should be placed in the cylinder, of course, and if the spell is done for diarrhea, it should be sewn in.

To cause constipation, plug the cylinder up at both ends and put it away in a dark place. If you wish, you can add a bit of yeast before you plug it up to cause bloating.

To cause diarrhea, put a string in one end of the cylinder then tie it to a tree branch and toss it in running water so that the water will run through the cylinder, but it will not float downstream.

Unplug the cylinder or remove it from water to break the spell.

If the cylinder is made to represent your enemy's throat, by naming it as such, other interesting things can be done. For instance, you can cause the person to choke or to suffer gastric reflux or vomiting.

DR. JOHANNES' DEAD FLIES FOR FACIAL DISCOMFORT

Fill a small bottle with dead flies and mineral oil. Let it sit for a minimum of three weeks, adding new dead flies as you acquire them. To cause discomfort, apply the oil to the face of your enemy by secretly smearing it onto his or her glasses frames, hairpins, the inside of a cap, or to a photo baptized in the person's name. A similar spell with equal discomfort can be made by making an oil with hairs from a rat instead of flies and using it in the same manner.

Read more about the Norse folk magic tradition in this book:
"Trolldom" by Johannes Bjorn Gardback

DEATH BY DEHYDRATION

Take a large, fresh, and healthy leaf from any plant or tree. With a fine-point marker (preferably black in colour), write the person's name and birth date on the leaf. Secure the leaf somewhere outside where it will be continuously exposed to the rays of the Sun. As the leaf dehydrates and withers away, so will the person. The remains will resemble ashes when crumbled. Throw the remains down the sewer, to the crossroads, or scatter them on a pathway near the person's trail.

CURSING IN A BOTTLE OR JAR

Container spells are found all around the world. In some cultures gourds and animal horns are the containers, but we Americans generally employ glass bottles and jars. Some containers are sealed to keep out air, in order to suffocate the enemy, while others call for a hole to be pieced in the lid, so that they can be turned upside down and the contents will slowly leak out.

These spells may be shaken and kept on an altar, hidden behind a toilet, thrown into running water, left at a crossroads, buried under a doorstep, hidden in a hollow tree, buried under or alongside a path, buried in a cemetery, or thrown over an enemy's roof.

Remember in all of these spells the overarching instruction to speak your curse and call your enemy's name aloud while preparing the work.

Read more about bottle spells here:
LuckyMojo.com/bottlespells.html by Catherine Yronwode

HOT FOOT IN A HOT SAUCE BOTTLE
To hot foot an enemy, write his name on a small slip of paper, then roll it tight and insert it into an unwashed bottle of strong, vinegary hot sauce. Drill or punch a small hole in the bottle cap and put it on the bottle. Take it to a river and throw it in. As the bottle floats downstream it will take on water and when it comes to rest, he will be forced to move away.

FOOTPRINT AND GOOFER DUST IN A JAR
Unlike other foot-track tricks, this one is contained in a jar. Gather the footprint of your enemy from the dirt and mix it up with a packet of Goofer Dust in a jar. Seal the jar tight. You may bury it on your enemy's property or under his doorstep to hold him down and keep him sick at home, or bury it in a cemetery to cause him to sicken and die.

GRAVEYARD DIRT AND COFFINS NAILS IN A JAR
To cause unnatural illness, injury, or misfortune, write your curse on the back of your enemy's photo and stab three coffin nails through the picture — for instance, in the two eyes and mouth, or in the head, heart, and genitals. Put the photo in a glass jar and add a packet of Graveyard Dirt and a dead insect. Close the jar and shake it up to distribute the ingredients. Place it in the hollow of a tree where the target passes frequently, or bury it.

DEAD SNAKE IN A JAR
Please do not kill a snake to perform this spell. Simply make use of one that is already dead. If you find a dead snake, at any time, take it home and put it in the freezer until you have a use for it. Once a picture and a personal concern of the enemy are acquired, write your command on the back of the picture. For instance, my command in this case might be, *"Rot away."* Put the paper and the personal concern into a glass jar, followed by the dead snake. Command that as the snake rots away, so will the target rot away. Put the lid back on the jar and seal. Bury it immediately on the enemy's property.

VINEGAR JAR TO CURSE AN ENEMY'S FORTUNE
This spell was first documented in *Hoodoo Herb and Root Magic* by Catherine Yronwode. "Write your enemy's name on brown paper with Dragon's Blood Ink and cross it out with a big black X. Wrap the name paper around a whole dried Red Pepper and tie it with a black thread. Submerge this packet into a jar of Four Thieves Vinegar and close the jar. For 13 consecutive nights during the waning Moon, burn a black candle dressed with Crossing Oil upside down, on the lid of the jar, always starting at an hour when both hands of the clock are falling (e.g. from 12:01 to 12:29). As you light the candle, speak aloud 13 justified curses, in your own words. Burn one candle per night, letting the wax from each candle build up on the jar's lid and sides. If you want to keep it going, stop after 13 days, wait out the period of the waxing Moon, and begin working it again when the Moon wanes."

DEATH IN A POTTED PLANT
Collect the Graveyard Dirt of someone who died badly — for example, in a terrible accident, from a drug overdose, or through suicide — and pay for it by leaving three dimes at the headstone. Write the name of the dead person and his birth and death dates on a small piece of paper. Write the name of your enemy on a matching piece of paper, giving his actual birth state, but today's date for his death. Pin the two papers together, facing one another, with four straight pins. Blend the Graveyard Dirt with potting soil. Half fill a nice plant pot with the soil mix, lay the papers in, set a house plant into the pot and pack it in with the soil mix. Water it well and give it as a present to your hated enemy.

DEACON MILLETT'S D.U.M.E. JAR SPELL

Deacon Millett, the author of *Hoodoo Honey and Sugar Spells,* is known as a kindly man, but when he works for justice, he pulls no punches. He is also a strong believer in technology, at least where images are concerned:

"The combination of words and pictures holds tremendous power. In cursing work, I use Photoshop image manipulation software to create damning images. One particular favourite, a collage of found images and personal photos, showed the enemy in a horrible auto accident, with the goddess Kali ripping the person's bleeding head off. This image was placed in a mason jar with Goofer Dust, smoked inside and out with D.U.M.E. Incense. Psalms 137 was prayed over the jar, which was labelled 'Death Unto My Enemy.' When I would come upon a Spider or Scorpion, I would put it inside the jar to die, just as the venomous foe deserved."

The smell inside the jar was horrible, and his victim, after two years of this treatment, met with a terrible tragedy. "Sometimes lightning strikes," he says, "And sometimes a curse takes a bit of time. Many people want a quick fix, which isn't always possible, but steady curses do take their toll."

ROOTWORKERS AND CHURCHES SPECIAL CURSE

Have you ever seen Lucky Mojo's 4 oz. Rootworkers and Churches Special? They are loaded to the extreme with herbs and minerals. A spell-caster's dream come true, they make our work so much easier if we wish to cast strong curses with minimal effort.

Each Rootworkers and Churches Special is custom made to the client's order, and you can select up to four different oils in your blend. Choose from among the titles on page 12 to suit your situation. Now, to make this into a powerful spell bottle, all you will need is a photo of your enemy's face, a personal concern of your enemy, and a roll of black duct tape.

First, remove the cap and pour out a little of the oil to prevent an overflow; use it to dress cursing candles or save it for use in other spells. Write your petition all over the picture in every direction, covering every area except the eyes. Draw an X over each eye. Roll the picture up into a tight cylinder and slip it in the bottle along with the personal concerns. Replace the cap. Wrap the entire bottle all over with duct tape. Bury it where the enemy will walk over it, or bury it in a cemetery.

Read more about Rootworkers and Churches Special oil blends here: **LuckyMojo.com/oilblends.html by Catherine Yronwode**

DESTRUCTION JAR

With a needle, inscribe thirteen black 6" candles from top-to-bottom in spiral fashion, with the word: "Destruction" for a total of 13 times. Anoint the candles with Destruction Oil from top to bottom. Wrap each candle in a triangle of paper and set them aside.

Write the enemy's name on a piece of paper, and cross it with the word "Destruction" written every which way, then dress the paper with Destruction Oil. Fold the enemy's personal concerns into the name paper and put the packet into a sturdy 16 oz. jar with a metal lid.

Pour a 4 oz. bottle of War Water into the jar, then put the empty War Water bottle in a plastic bag and smash it with a hammer. Empty the glass shards into the jar. Do the same with a 4 oz. bottle of Four Thieves Vinegar and a 4 oz. bottle of Habanero hot sauce.

Add nine coffin nails, nine pins, nine needles, nine razor blades. Then add Poppy Seed, Red Pepper flakes, Black Mustard Seed, Goofer Dust, and Graveyard Dirt. Top this mess off with spoiled and soured milk. State your curse as many times as possible while you work.

Before placing the lid on the bottle, smear a gelled glue, like Goop, Gorilla Glue, or Crazy Glue, on the inside lip of the lid or the threads of the jar. This is to prevent the gases from the contents forcing the lid off. Once the lid is on and the glue sets, shake the jar vigorously.

Burn one candle on the lid each night for 13 nights. Shake the jar as much as possible when candles are not being used. Keep the jar behind the toilet between candle-burning sessions. Be careful: it may explode.

CROOKED ROOTS AND STILL WATER

In 1937 a Spiritualist in Washington, D.C., told Rev. Hyatt that in 1916 he had been hurt by a woman named Lucy Williams. She had gotten the seat of his underwear and part of his left sock, and packed them into a square whiskey bottle with crooked roots and still water, that is, water which she had let sit for nine days. After assembling the bottle, she had worked over it for nine days and then she had buried it. As a result, the man became bent over. He had no aches or pains, but he could not stand up straight.

Mary Moody, a worker in Richmond, Virginia, told him that the bottle was buried by his path, and when he found it and dug it up, she asked for a picture of Lucy Williams, placed the photo in front of the bottle, drew a pistol, and shot through the photo, breaking the bottle. The man was cured.

CURSING WITH CANDLES

CANDLES AS HELPER LIGHTS

Some workers believe there is a veil between our world and the Spirit world. They say the flame of a candle will pierce that veil and allow us access to the entities on the other side. My personal thought is, "The more candles, the better!" and I set the number of candles that I personally correlate to each type of spell. For instance, the numbers 9 and 13 represent cursing to me, so that is the number of candles I use in my curses. The total may consist of one or more vigils plus a number of 4" or 6" helper lights. I inscribe the curse into each helper light, in spiral fashion, top-to-bottom, dress it with cursing oil, and set a petition under each one.

I also like the Candle Ministry services at Missionary Independent Spiritual Church. they will set vigil lights to back up your work at home:
CandleMinistry.com

DARKNESS AT NOON

Rev. Hyatt was taught this curse in Saint Petersburg, Florida, in 1939.

"The black candle is for evil. That black candle does all the harm in the world. Say, if you wanted to do someone harm, then at twelve o'clock noon, make it no later, you go into your room and pull your blinds down. You set a black taper candle behind you, and you set your face pointing to the East.

"You haven't got a picture; you set there in the dark until your mind just kind of pictures the person. And say, if you want to cause them to get killed some way, by running into a train, or by landing where the train can run over them, well, just what you want, that thing that you want to have happen, why, you just picture that and call it aloud, and that black candle will be burning behind you, and you call that person's name nine times.

"Then you cross them. You take your two fingers and cross them like an X, these two big index fingers. Crook them tight and then pull them apart, hard — Unnh! — as you say, *'To Hell, to Hell, you go. Drift forever. No contentment. There's no rest for the weary,'* or what you pictured to happen.

"And then you turn and blow the candle out and get on the floor and kneel in front of it and say, *"I ask for six feet."* That's the depth they bury the coffin. That gives that candle time to cool off. You ask for it slowly, *'S-i-i-i-x f-e-e-e-t.'* By then, all the smoke from that candle will blow off. Then you wrap the candle up for next time, and go on about your business."

SEVEN DAY CANDLE CURSE TO TAKE AWAY ALL

This spell is a favourite of Professor Charles Porterfield:

"To destroy someone and take everything they have away from them, get six black 6" candles and one white 6" candle. Using a coffin nail, carve the name of the person you wish to harm onto the first black candle. On the second black candle, carve his name and the word 'Job.' On the third black candle, carve his name and the word 'Wealth.' On the fourth black candle, carve his name and the word 'Car.' On the fifth black candle, carve his name and the word 'Happiness.' On the sixth black candle, carve his name and the word 'Health.' Using a pin, carve your own name on the white, seventh candle.

"Set the candles out in a row with the black candles first and the white candle last. Dress the black candles with an equal mixture of Confusion and Jinx Oil and then dust them with D.U.M.E. Sachet Powder. Dress the white candle with Hyssop Oil and dust it with Blessing Sachet Powder.

"At midnight on Saturday night, call your curse, light the first black candle, and let it burn until it is finished. Repeat each night at midnight, burning the remaining five black candles on Sunday, Monday, Tuesday, Wednesday, and Thursday, and calling the curses specific to those candles.

"Finally, to break the pattern of lighting candles at midnight, at noon on Friday, light the blessed white candle and pray Psalms 51 over it.

"Dispose of any spell remains at a crossroads."

GIRL, GO AWAY!

This spell comes from Susan Barnes:

"If a female co-worker is flirting with your man, get a pretty neck scarf, dust it lightly with Banishing Powder, and scream, *"Jane Doe, GO AWAY"* On a black candle, inscribe her name nine times. On top of the names write, 'Go Away!' 'Stay away!' 'Leave my man alone!" Light the candle, placing the tricked scarf near it. Three times, as the candle is burning, scream at the scarf, and call her name. Picture her leaving the office, leaving your man, or leaving the town, never to return. Pray Psalms 53 for shutting up enemies and filling them with fear. She will become quiet, fearful, and want to leave. As the candle finishes, burn her business card or her photo to ashes. Throw the wax remains and ashes in a moving river and yell, *'Jane Doe, GO FAR AWAY! Be Gone!'* Place the tricked scarf in a gift box and give it to her with a smile, telling her that you think the colours will look pretty on her."

A SATANIC CANDLE SPELL TO CURSE AN ENEMY

This curse comes from the Grand Mufti of Satanism:

"If you desire that someone should suffer, endure torment, be stricken with illness, and then eventually die as a result, curse them in the following manner:

"Begin this spell on the Dark Moon, preferably on a Saturday. It is best done out of doors, at a wilderness crossroads at midnight or 3:00 AM where and when no one will disturb you.

"Obtain a black devil figural candle, a palm-sized photograph of the victim, a dish large enough to hold the candle resting atop the photo, a rusty coffin nail, a handful of pins, and a bottle of War Water.

"Using the coffin nail, carve on the back of the candle the words: *'YOU ARE CURSED, YOU DOOMED ASSHOLE'* or some other vitriolic expression of your hatred and malice.

"Take pins and cross them through the enemy's eyes on the photo, through her mouth, her heart, crotch and any other areas desired, saying, *'Blind and muted, pain be yours, repugnant idiot! Diseases and sexless suffering overtake you!'* Be creative and curse every body part by name as you stick a pin through it.

"Set the photo face-down in the dish and pour in some War Water. Grasp the devil candle and exhort, *'Devil take this warty moron and torture her, maim her! Give her a slow, painful death!'*

"Light the candle and laugh triumphantly, setting the candle on the photo to initiate the curse. After 13 minutes, pinch out the flame and leave the mess there until your return, or hide it nearby.

"On successive Tuesdays or Saturdays, the days of Mars and Saturn, light the candle for 13 minutes, add a bit more War Water and verbally curse her with maladies and worsening health.

"To intensify the spell, piss into the dish, then remove the candle, defecate into it, and replace the candle into the terrible muck.

"Once the candle finally sputters out, drowned in the hoary goo, exclaim triumphantly, *'VICTORY IS MINE! ONLY DEATH WILL BE YOUR RELEASE!'*

"Bury the mess in the grave of a disease victim or an insane murderer, consigning your enemy to the unfortunate or evil one's care."

You can read more Satanic spells, rituals, and fatwas in this book:

"The Gospel of Satan" by Troll Towelhead

SKULL CANDLE SPELLS

Skull candles look pretty intimidating, don't they? Let's face it, they are both ugly and scary in appearance. Decades ago, after having seen a skull candle for the first time, I had to take a step back: CREEPY!

But, as a Registered Nurse, this candle deeply aroused my curiosity. After having examined the matter in greater detail, I realized what the skull candle actually represented: the human mind!

Following that revelation, it occurred to me that whoever invented the skull candle was a creative genius! I do not know who it was, but I do know that skull candles appeared in mail order hoodoo catalogues as long ago as World War Two, and they have been popular ever since.

Before we start lighting candles, let's familiarize ourselves what the Mayfield Clinic of Cincinnati, Ohio, calls "...an amazing three-pound organ that controls all functions of the body, interprets information from the outside world, and embodies the essence of the mind and soul."

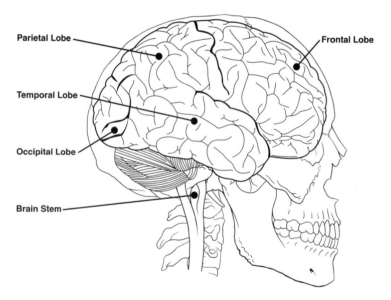

The human brain, showing the major lobes and their position within the skull. As you work with skull candles, keep this image in mind, and inflict damage and pain where most appropriate. Art by Greywolf Townsend.

THE FUNCTION OF THE LOBES AND THE BRAIN STEM

The lobes of the brain, along with the brain stem, are the areas that we will be working with as we curse the skull candle.

Please take a look at the diagram of the brain on the opposite page to see exactly where each of the lobes is located. Then read through these descriptions of the functions of the lobes, as explained here according to information supplied by the Mayfield Clinic:

Frontal Lobe
- Personality, behaviours, and emotions
- Judgement, planning, and problem solving
- Speaking and writing
- Body movement
- Intelligence, concentration, and self-awareness

Parietal Lobe
- Interpreting language and words
- Senses of touch, pain, and temperature
- Interpreting visual, auditory, motor, sensory, and memory signals

Occipital Lobe
- Interpreting vision, including colour, light, and movement

Temporal Lobe
- Understanding language
- Memory
- Hearing
- Sequencing and organization

The Brain Stem
- Breathing and heart rate
- Body temperature
- Cycles of waking and sleeping
- Sneezing
- Coughing
- Swallowing
- Digestion and vomiting

RIGHT BRAIN, LEFT BRAIN, LOBES, AND BRAIN STEM

The right and left hemispheres of the brain are joined by a bundle of fibers that deliver messages from one side to the other. Each hemisphere controls the opposite side of the body, so that if a tumour, stroke, or traumatic brain injury is located on the right side of a person's brain, her left arm or leg may be weak or paralyzed. Keep this in mind as you curse with skull candles: An injury to the brain will be manifested on the opposite site of the body.

In addition, the left hemisphere controls speech, comprehension, arithmetic, and writing. The left hemisphere is dominant in hand use and language in about 92% of people.

The right hemisphere controls creativity, spatial ability, artistry, and musical skills. The right hemisphere is dominant in about 8% of people.

As previously noted, the brain is also divided into several lobes — the frontal, parietal, temporal, and occipital lobes — each with its own set of functions. At the base of the brain, the brain stem consists of three structures, the midbrain, pons, and medulla. This area acts as a relay center between the brain and the spinal cord. It performs many automatic functions of the body of which we may not be entirely conscious.

GETTING STARTED WITH SKULL CANDLES

Figural candles, also called image candles, are made in the form of whatever we, as spell-casters, wish to manipulate. Figural candles are preferred by many practitioners when working unusual or extremely strong spells, because their visual symbolism is easy to see, in what amounts to a cross between working with candles and working with doll-babies. Therefore, you will see skull candles, as well as other types of figural candles, treated in ways similar to the spell suggestions that are given in the doll-baby portion of this book.

The skull candle is one of my most effective spell-casting tools, second only to the doll-baby. Why? Because the human brain controls everything in the lives of our enemies — and if we, as rootworkers, are familiar with some of the brain functions, we can control their minds to an extent and also inflict various ideas, thoughts, and physical ailments upon them.

It is preferred to work with black skull candles for cursing work. If a black candle is not available, then a white candle will suffice because white is a neutral colour and can be used in lieu of any other colour.

NAMING AND BAPTIZING THE SKULL CANDLE

There are numerous ways to work with skull candles. But, no matter what colour is used or what spell is performed, the very first steps are to baptize and name it. Often figural candles are inscribed, loaded, and dressed prior to naming and baptizing, but, for cursing purposes, we want the enemy to feel the pain of any little thing that we do, and this is why I recommend bringing life to the candle as the first step.

INSCRIBING THE SKULL CANDLE

If we do not wish to load the candle, then it should be inscribed at this time. However, if we plan to load it with a name paper, petition, personal concerns, or cursing materials, then the inscription process will be performed after the candle has been loaded and sealed.

All that is needed is a pencil, pin, needle, knife point, Cactus spine, thorn, or coffin nail to write the inscription. The writing need not be neat and it need not even be legible after it has been written into the wax. In addition to the usual inscriptions, such as the name, birth date, and a wish or petition, a skull candle allows us to locate multiple commands on it, based on which portions of the brain, and thus our victim's mind, we are seeking to influence.

In the three examples that follow, it will help if you first refer to the page that describes the lobes and the brain stem, with the correlating human functions that they control, and then locate those areas on the illustration of the parts of the brain.

First, consider the frontal lobe. It controls functions such as personality, behaviours, emotions, judgement, and problem solving. So, if we want to mess up a co-worker on the job to get her fired, or cause a hostile witness to misspeak at a court trial, you could simply inscribe, directly over the frontal lobe, the word "Confusion."

Next, look at the brain stem. It controls breathing, heart rate, and other life forces. So to kill an enemy or make him ill, you could inscribe, directly over the brainstem, words like "Death," "Cardiac Arrest," "Vomiting," to induce negative outcomes related to that portion of the brain.

Finally, consider the temporal lobe. Among its many functions, it controls memory. You could inscribe "Forget!" on that region of the skull to keep a rival or slanderer from bringing up your past or to keep an enemy from recalling your password and hacking your social media account.

LOADING THE SKULL CANDLE

Prior to loading any candle, we have to remove some wax from it in order to access its interior.

Many people use a knife point to dig out a small divot of wax, load the candle, melt the dug-out wax in a soup ladle, and pour it back in. This traditional method is not bad, but I know some better ways.

I used to drill holes into the skull candles with a power drill prior to loading them with papers, herbs, minerals, Goofer Dust, Ants, and Fly Maggots. I still consider this a viable option because it allows me to inflict severe headaches on my victim.

However, I now find it a lot easier and faster to work with a soldering iron. These can be purchased from any hardware store at an average price range of $10.00 - $20.00. If a soldering iron is your tool of choice, please work outdoors, as this tool emits harmful fumes.

We need to save the wax drippings to seal the load in the candle, so have a metal collection unit, such as a loaf pan, nearby. Additionally, a metal funnel is handy for loading and sealing the candle.

Hold the candle over the collection unit and burrow the holes into it. It is a lot faster to craft all the holes at one time rather than burrowing a hole, stuffing it, sealing it, and going to the next one.

To decide where to place the holes and what to insert into them, refer to the page describing the lobes of the brain and their correlating functions. A personal concern of the enemy ought to be inserted into one of the holes, but the location of the rest, and the materials loaded into them, are entirely up to you. These examples may help as you learn the work:

Using the previous idea of harming the frontal lobe for confusion, we can intensify that effect by loading the frontal lobe hole with Poppy Seeds, dead Crazy Ants, and Marijuana to diminish the power of judgement. Add a tiny petition paper for "Confusion." (A large paper can cause a huge fire if the candle flame meets it.) Seal the hole, then inscribe "Confusion" on it.

Goofer Dust is appropriate for the brain stem, as it controls life forces.

The temporal lobes, which control memory and language, will respond well to Stop Gossip or Do As I Say Incense.

Crossing Incense works well in any of the lobes.

I am especially fond of placing incense both inside and outside of the candle because when the fire of the candle flame consumes it, the incense sends even more messages to the Spirit world.

SEALING THE HOLES IN THE SKULL CANDLE

Although all the holes are made at one time, loading and sealing them is best done one hole at a time, to prevent spillage. After stuffing, seal the hole with warm wax. Just place the metal collection unit on a stove and heat the wax at a low setting. Then, spoon the wax into the hole, funnel it in, or use a cooking syringe to fill and seal the hole. If you did not previously inscribe the candle, this is the time to do so.

ANOINTING THE SKULL CANDLE AND PETITION PAPER

Dress the entire skull candle with your chosen cursing oil or oil blend. Start at the top of the candle and move downward to the base.

If you have a picture and/or a petition paper to be placed under the candle, dab it in a 5-spot pattern with your cursing oil. Sprinkle herbs, powders, or incense on it, and fold it up or leave it flat, as you choose.

ROLLING, DUSTING, OR DRESSING THE SKULL CANDLE

After anointing the skull candle with oil, immediately roll it in powdered cursing ingredients or dust it by sprinkling or blowing powders on it. Immediacy is important because a newly anointed candle is moist and sticky, allowing the cursing ingredients to adhere to it.

Powders to use include any cursing incense, alone or mixed with herbs; Goofer Dust alone or mixed with incense or herbs. Sachet powders are better blown onto candles than used for rolling them in,

Optionally, after anointing and dressing the skull candle, rub dog or chicken feces all over its face, like makeup. While doing this, state that everyone who looks at the person will see nothing but a piece of shit. Be sure to wear gloves while performing this operation.

STICKING THE SKULL CANDLE

If desired, heat up 50 to 100 pins, a packet of needles, a packet of coffin nails, or a dozen razor blades and stick them into the candle, leaving them standing up like hair. If you are neat, you can place the rows of pins in a grid and call your curse 50 to 100 times as you do so.

FIRE SAFETY WITH THE SKULL CANDLE

To prevent fires, cover the altar with sand. Place pebble-sized stones on the sand. Put the candle in a metal pie plate and set it on the pebbles.

D.U.M.E. SKULL CANDLE SPELL

Now you can put all you have learned about skull candles to work.

Baptize and name a black skull candle. Go outside with your soldering iron and metal collection unit. Burrow one hole into each of the lobes and into the brain stem, and collect the wax. Turn the soldering iron off and return inside.

Make a mixture of D.U.M.E. Incense, a vial's worth of dead Ants, dead Maggots collected from feces, Poppy Seeds, Vandal Root, Goofer Dust, and Graveyard Dirt.

Use your funnel to fill one hole. Warm the wax to the melting point, aspirate some of it into your syringe, and fill the hole with the melted wax. Repeat this process for each hole. Add two very small pieces of paper that have the word: "Death" written on them into the brainstem hole and the frontal lobe hole. Personal concerns can go into the brainstem. Add Red Pepper to the parietal lobes and place any addictive substances, if available, into the temporal lobes.

When the holes are all sealed and the wax is stiff, inscribe the candle, anoint it with D.U.M.E. Oil, and roll it in the remaining herb mixture.

With tongs, heat the tips of nine coffin nails and an assortment of pins and needles and stick them into the lobes, brainstem, eyeballs, and ears.

Write a curse on the enemy's photo and dab it with D.U.M.E. Oil in a 5-spot pattern. Place it face-upward on a metal pie plate and set the candle on it. Light the candle and scream your curses once an hour as it burns.

BLACK SKULL CANDLE TO DRIVE OFF YOUR EX

This spell is intended to cut off a pestiferous or stalking ex-lover.

Name and baptize a black skull candle and rub it all over with Black Arts Oil. Do not light it yet, but rub oil on it every night for nine nights. On the ninth night, dust the candle with Hot Foot Incense, light it, and use its flame to heat up nine coffin nails, one at a time. As each nail becomes hot at the tip, drive it into one of the nine vulnerable areas of the head.

First stab the two eyes, saying, *"John Doe, you can no longer see me."* Then the two ears: *"John Doe, you can no longer hear me."* Then the two nostrils: *"John Doe, you can no longer smell me."* Then the mouth: *"John Doe, you can no longer speak to me."* Next is the center of the forehead or frontal lobe: *"John Doe, you can no longer think of me."* And finally, stab the brainstem, saying, *"John Doe, it's death to you if you bother me again."*

THE CALIGULA SPELL WITH A SKULL CANDLE

Caligula was a ruthless ancient Roman emperor who stopped at nothing to torture his enemies. One of his techniques was to bury victims, alive, up to their necks. That way, the victims could see their impending doom while Caligula enjoyed watching the fear on their faces as he subjected them to a slow, horrendous torture.

Sometimes, the lions came out. Would a lion munch on their heads for a very painful and lingering death? Or would the gladiators, on their chariots, playing a form of golf with their heads, kill them? Would the blows be an instant decapitated death or a lingering one? HORRIBLE!

So, let Caligula be our role model and let's perform similar torture techniques on our enemy.

Note that in this spell the candle is not burned; it is treated as if it were a doll-baby or effigy.

Prepare the skull candle. Either bury outside or in a pot up to the bridge of the nose so that the eyes are exposed. Insure that it will be exposed to direct sunlight when outside, as this is a form of dehydrating the enemy. When passing by it, pour a little boiling water on the candle. Throw dog defecation on it! If there is privacy, urinate on it! Step on it! Throw rocks at it! If there are gardening or lawn tools around, poke it in the eyes or slice a piece of it! Remember to scream your curses at it each and every time that it is tortured.

Once it's pretty roughed up and nothing is visible, we can remove it from the dirt, and perform the next spell.

BEAT TO DEATH

This is my variation of a revenge spell that I got from Catherine Yronwode, who learned it from Papa Jim Sickafus of San Antonio, Texas, about 30 years ago. The candle is used as an effigy and not burned.

Prepare a skull candle — or, better, use the one left over from the Caligula spell above. Wrap the entire candle in Blackberry leaves, then in a piece of black cloth. Use duct tape generously to enclose all of it in duct tape until it is completely encased. With a hammer, beat the Hell out of it every day, for 7 days, calling your desire for revenge each day. When done, bury it in a deep hole or throw it into a sewer.

Read more revenge spells at the Lucky Mojo Esoteric Archive:
LuckyMojo.com/spells/black/revengespells.html

CURSING WITH DOLL-BABIES AND EFFIGIES

For many workers, an effigy doll provides the ultimate form of domination, especially if it is made with personal concerns to give us a spiritual link to the person we are cursing, and if we baptize it and call our victim's essence or spirit into the doll as we bring it to life. If well made and used with conviction, the person represented by the doll will become completely helpless and defenseless against whatever we may do to it.

Doll-baby is the most common name for these dolls in hoodoo, but they are also called Voodoo dolls (from Haitian practice) and poppets (from European practice). All these terms refer to the same thing.

Not all curses employ dolls, but those that do often require that the doll be prepared ahead of time. They can be created from many materials:

• **Bread and Bread Dough**
• **Broom Straw**
• **Clay and Mud**
• **Cloth and Clothing of the Enemy**
• **Corn Husks**
• **Feathers**
• **Figural Candles**
• **Leather**
• **Meat and Fat**
• **Metal, either cast or sheet**
• **Paper, Index Stock, Chipboard, and Cardboard**
• **Photographs, Silhouettes, or Drawings of the Enemy**
• **Play Dough**
• **Rope**
• **Roots**
• **Spanish Moss**
• **Steamed Rice**
• **Straw**
• **String**
• **Toy Dolls made of Porcelain, Cloth, Rubber, Wood, or Plastic**
• **Twigs and Sticks**
• **Wax**
• **Wood**

MAKING A CLOTH DOLL

Because personal concerns have an inherent magical link to the one with whom they have been in contact, some workers prefer to hand-sew cursing dolls from the underwear, socks, or clothing of their victims. The closer the clothing was worn to the victim's skin, the better, and, of course, unwashed or soiled clothes are preferred to those that are freshly laundered.

If you cannot obtain the clothing of the victim, you can purchase a cloth doll or sew one yourself. Black cloth is a common choice.

Patterns for flat dolls can be found online. You do not need a machine; just hand-sew it. Leave the head open to stuff the doll.

After turning the doll seam-side-in, put personal concerns in it, if you have them, trying to keep them in the appropriate part of the doll's body. For example, toenails would go in the feet, pubic hair would go at the genitals, and head hair would go in the head.

You may also add a name paper with the person's birthdate and a cursing petition paper. Some workers enclose a photo of the victim within the doll, others prefer to glue a photo of the face onto the doll's head. You may embroider facial features, if you wish. Using an X for each eye and a turned-down mouth is traditional on a cursing doll.

Fill the doll with cursing herbs, roots, minerals, and insects. Goofer Dust can be added as well. If the doll still feels a little skimpy, use a cursing incense powder, straw, or Spanish Moss to fill it out.

Spanish Moss may be left sticking out of the head, to give the doll some hair, if wanted. Finish by closing up the head with whip-stitching.

MS. ROBIN'S TIPS ON HOW TO STUFF A CLOTH DOLL

Ms. Robin is an experienced worker who teaches classes on cursing with dolls. She says, "The location of the items within the doll will affect the body parts with which they come into contact, and the specific stuffing items are selected on the basis of how they will affect the doll. For instance, placing Red Peppers in the feet will give the doll a case of 'hot foot' and stuffing Poppy Seeds in the head will confuse the person in thought and speech. Likewise, placing Vandal Root in the doll's arm pits will result in bad body odour, but when placed in the mouth area, Vandal Root will give the person bad breath."

Read the text of Ms. Robin's class on cursing with dolls in this book: **"The Black Folder" edited by Catherine Yronwode**

MAKING A CLAY DOLL

While the cloth doll is ideal for delivering beatings, as well as being easy to anguish with pins, needles, razor blades, and nails, the clay doll works well for torture methods such as burnings, prolonged exposure to moisture, and amputations without risking spillage of the contents. I am especially fond of this type of doll because it can be immersed in a container of fresh, stinking dog feces.

To make a truly personalized clay doll, purchase a packet of air-drying clay at a crafts store. Divide the clay into four sections: one for the back torso, one for the front torso (and breasts if it is female), one for the legs (and penis if it is a male), and one for the arms and head. Place all four pieces in warm water to prevent rapid drying, which will happen once the clay is taken out of the package.

Set out several layers of paper towels on a flat surface to absorb the moisture that the clay will take up from the warm water. Have enough towels so that each piece of clay can be handled over fresh paper towels.

The first piece of clay is used to make the back portion of the torso. This will be the foundation of the doll. Knead it flat until there is enough clay surface to contain all the personal concerns and the various cursing ingredients to be used. With a pencil, inscribe your victim's name and birthdate into the clay.

Use the second piece of clay to roll out two short, sturdy legs, and a penis if the victim is male. Graft the top portions of the legs and penis into the foundation.

Use the third piece of clay to make arms, a thick neck, and a head, and smoothly graft this into the foundation.

Use the fourth piece of clay to form the front torso, with breasts, if the victim is female. Make it just slightly smaller than the back torso. Inscribe the enemy's name and birthdate on this portion also, and set it aside.

Next, place the personal concerns, petition paper, name paper, and herbal or powdered cursing ingredients over the foundation portion of the doll. Top this with the front section of clay. Fold the foundation up and over the front section and smooth the surface of the entire doll until there are no visible seams. If the name and birthdate are not visible after this work, you may inscribe them on the front of the torso again.

The drying period is time-consuming. Rest the doll on fresh layers of paper towels and turn it at least once a day until it is completely dry.

MAKING A WAX OR FAT DOLL

Wax and fat remain soft, so you can knead the herbs or powders right into the body as you form the doll. These dolls are great for melting away while reciting Psalms 37: (*"The wicked shall perish, and the enemies of the Lord shall be as the fat of lambs: they shall consume; into smoke shall they consume away"*).

MAKING A BREAD DOUGH DOLL

Mud, steamed rice, bread, or bread dough are soft, so to harden the outer surface, bake them in a kitchen oven. Bread dolls made with non-toxic ingredients may be fed to the dogs when the enemy is a female. Recite 2 Kings 9: (*"And the dogs shall eat Jezebel ... and there shall be none to bury her. ... In the portion of Jezreel shall dogs eat the flesh of Jezebel: And the carcass of Jezebel shall be as dung upon the face of the field in the portion of Jezreel; so that they shall not say, This is Jezebel"*).

MAKING A TWIG OR ROOT DOLL

Stick, twig, root, straw, and feather dolls are made by binding the items together with thread or string. They may be given a simple poncho-like garment to wear and the load of personal concerns and cursing herbs is often placed in a shoulder-bag for them to carry.

MAKING A ROPE DOLL

Rope dolls are made by binding short lengths of rope together with thread. They are dressed and loaded like twig dolls.

MAKING A CORN HUSK DOLL

Soak the corn husks overnight to make them flexible, then fold and tie them into a human shape with the load inside. When they dry they will be flammable and are thus used in spells where fire is the torture tool.

MAKING A PAPER DOLL

Photos or silhouettes of paper, cardboard, or metal can be used as-is, or doubled, with personal concerns and herbs glued between the layers.

Read more about how to make and use folkloric dolls in this book:
"The Black Folder" edited by Catherine Yronwode

NAMING AND BAPTIZING A CURSING DOLL

Having made our doll-baby, next we bring it to life. This can be accomplished simply blowing breath into the doll's mouth and nostrils followed by naming it.

All effigies must be told who they are. This is accomplished by naming or baptizing them. In addition to linking the effigy to the enemy, the act of naming also summons a spark or essence of the enemy's spirit into the effigy, creating a vulnerability in the enemy that we can exploit.

There are many ways to name a photo or a doll. If my enemy's name is John Doe, I could write the name and birthdate on a photo or use a needle to inscribe a figural candle, hold the item in my hands, and say, *"I name you John Doe."* I could hold the doll in my left hand, make the sign of the cross with my right hand, and say, *"In the name of the Father, the Son, and The Holy Ghost, I name you John Doe."* However, due to my own spiritual background and religious training, my rites are a little more elaborate:

I first anoint the doll. You may use water, whiskey, Florida Water, or Holy Water, but I personally prefer Lucky Mojo 7-11 Holy Oil, a Biblical formula compounded according to an ancient recipe.

I dip my right index and middle fingers into the oil, hold the doll in my left hand, and make the sign of the cross on and over it while saying, out loud: *"I baptize you in the name of the Father, the Son, and the Holy Spirit. Amen."* The image will have a cross of oil on it.

Next, I hold the image in both of my hands and envision my victim. Then I hold it up into the air, toward the sky, with both hands, while envisioning electrical sparks or lightning coming from my shoulders, through my arms and my hands, and into the doll. I then scream: *"And I name you John Doe, John Doe, John Doe..."* calling out the name nine times — a thoroughly effective ritual!

Read a variety of doll-naming and baptismal rituals online here: **LuckyMojo.com/spells/practicaltips.html#doll by CatYronwode**

ESTABLISHING A RELATIONSHIP WITH THE DOLL

Ensure that with each interaction you make dominating eye contact with the doll, maintaining an ongoing authoritative position and a commanding voice tone. It is not a good idea to work the doll if sleepy, or feeling tranquil or mellow. Instead, be angry, always remembering the damage that your enemy has caused.

CURSING THE DOLL BY BODY PART

It is traditional to use 13 pins to stab a doll, but the places they are inserted may vary. The results they are intended to produce, are as follows:

- **Head:** headaches, cerebral stroke
- **Eyes:** blindness
- **Ears:** deafness, ringing in the ears
- **Mouth:** silence, tooth decay
- **Hands:** inability to hit anyone
- **Stomach:** ulcers, vomiting, stomach cancer
- **Intestines:** gastritis, colon cancer
- **Kidneys:** kidney stones
- **Uterus:** sterility, miscarriage
- **Genitals:** painful intercourse, impotence
- **Anus:** hemorrhoids, piles
- **Hips and Knees:** arthritis
- **Feet:** swelling, inability to run away or leave

TORTURING A CLAY DOLL

Here are some of my favourite techniques for torturing clay dolls:

- **Amputations:** Taking a saw and cutting off a foot, arm, leg, or penis works well with this type of doll.
- **War Water or Vinegar:** These fluids can be thrown on the face or body of the doll or it can be drowned in these fluids.
- **Soldering Iron:** Applying intense heat to a body part will be painful! I like to apply the soldering iron to the genitals, anus, eyes, or ears.
- **Lighter or Match:** Burn areas of the body just to create pain without creating total combustion of the doll. The best areas for this are the soles of the feet.
- **Barbeque Grill:** Turn on the barbeque grill until it is well singed.
- **Storage:** I like to collect large amounts of fresh dog feces in a large clay container. I place the doll face-down in the dog feces, just half way, to make the doll suffocate in the disgust of dog shit. In the summertime, I leave this container uncovered and water it to keep it moist and to attract flies. The flies will lay eggs and maggots will emerge and crawl all over the doll.

TORTURING A CLOTH DOLL

Here are some of my favourite techniques of inflicting damage on cloth and other pliable dolls:

- **Binding:** Use duct tape or string to bind the doll by taping or tying its legs and hands together.
- **Cutting:** Cut the doll with broken glass or razor blades.
- **Stabbing:** Stick coffins nails, pins, needles, and tacks into the doll. Use a staple gun and aim for the genitals, the nipples, the eye balls! Jab it repeatedly with a knife or an ice pick. Do it fast and do it slow. Imagine your enemy in front of you and hear his screams.
- **Bludgeoning:** Take a hammer and pound the shit out of its body parts, either all over or in one area, such as the knees. If outside, throw heavy rocks at it to stone it to death! Slam that son-of-a-bitch with a board or a baseball bat while commanding it to suffer.
- **Drilling:** Use an electric drill to bore holes into the doll.
- **Strangulation:** Strangle it with thin wires or thread while seeing your enemy struggling to breathe!
- **Hanging:** Wrap wire, rope, or string around the doll's neck and hang it from a tree. ConjureMan Ali hangs cursing dolls on the blades of a ceiling fan and sets it to spin at slow speed to make the victim dizzy.
- **Dog Attack:** Provoke a pet dog to growl and show its teeth at the doll to scare your foe. Don't let the dog bite into the doll if there are the harmful contents inside or outside of it, but consider giving a non-toxic doll to the dog as a chew-toy.
- **Storage:** When the cloth doll is not in use, store it in a box that contains plenty of moth balls, forcing your victim to lay with poisons. Place a mirror over the doll's face so that everything evil that the enemy does will bounce right back to her.

THE FINALE: MURDERING AND BURYING THE DOLL

Killing the doll is a common practice when the work of torture is complete. The many ways to do this include burning it to ashes, melting it, drowning it in a body of water, dismembering it, hammering it to pieces, and burying it in a cemetery within a coffin or directly in the ground.

In the chapter on mirrors, you will learn how to make a coffin for the doll that serves the dual purpose of reversing evil as well as burial.

BURYING AN OLD COW'S TONGUE AS A DOLL

The female root doctor whom Rev. Hyatt met in Memphis, Tennessee, in 1939 and called "Informant 1520" gave this amazing doll spell: "Well, just like you want to put someone to a slow death. You go to the — I don't know whether you can get them at the grocery store — anyhow, you go where they kill beef. You get you an old beef tongue meat, let the cow be old, old as you can — one of them long tongues. And you lay that tongue down just like someone laying down dead here. You get you a brand-new pocket knife, ain't never been used. You get hold of that knife and say, *'Son-of-bitch, die, die.'* Drive the knife in and say, *'Son of-a-bitch, die, die, dwindle away, can't stay here, can't stay nowhere, until you're dead.'* You cut it in half lengthwise and you go to their front gate and you dig a hole there, outside their gate and you bury it just like a grave, and you build it like a grave, mound and tombstone over it. And when that tongue rots, he either fall from a stroke or dwindle away, but he's gone."

NATHEN STEININGER'S SPIRIT TRAP DOLL BY A RIVER

Get a small muslin bag and some personal concerns of the enemy. Fill the bag with Couch Grass, Dogsbane, Knotweed and Mullein. Place the personal concerns as close to the center of the bag as possible.

Anoint a black 6" candle with Come To Me Oil and Controlling Oil. (This is an unusual use for Come To Me Oil.) Sprinkle a circle of Tobacco around the candle. Sit facing the direction of your enemy while he is asleep. Light the candle and call to the spirit of the person, asking it to come to you and directing it into the bag. Once you have lured the enemy's spirit into the bag, pull it shut and tie it closed. Let the candle burn itself out.

Make a doll out of the bag by pinching part of it near the top and tying it to make a little head shape. Name the doll for the person you are cursing. Anoint it with Confusion Oil and Destruction Oil or Crossing Oil. Put the doll in a small wooden box. Place stones over it and fill the rest of box with Goofer Dust or dirt from a cemetery.

Take this box to a river, and bury it deeply along the river bank close to where the water and land meet. Place a heavy stone on top to hold it down. As you bury the box, speak to it, telling the spirit you trapped in the box that this is its new home. Curse the spirit to wander this river eternally. This will affect the person while he or she still lives and, if God wills it, after death the spirit will be trapped along the river bank as well.

BLINDING AND SUFFOCATING A CLOTH DOLL

Make a black fabric doll and fill it with Rat poison; cursing powders; cursing herbs, minerals, and roots; personal concerns; mouldy bread; raw meat, a photo of the enemy and your curse. Stuff it with Spanish Moss for added volume, state your curse again to the Spanish Moss. Stitch the doll closed at the last seam. Stick coffin nails into its eyes, the back of neck (in the brain stem), genital area, and rectum.

Next, generously pour the cursing oil on its eyes, nose, mouth, ears, head, stomach, genitals, and rectum. Insure that your intent is stated aloud and that it is specific to each body part being cursed. For example, when pouring oil into the eyes, say, *"You will have blindness,"* when pouring on the nose and mouth, say, *"You won't be able to breathe,"* and so on.

Finally, duct tape the Hell out of the doll by binding its hands, feet, and mouth. Keep it outside of the house because you will encourage the mould to grow and the meat to rot, creating a stench. Beat the doll on a regular basis with a hammer and throw water on it to encourage mould growth. If your enemy is a drinker, throw beer on it; if a diabetic, sprinkle it with sugar. After it rots, deploy it in running water or bury it.

PROFESSOR AMES' KILLER WAX DOLL-BABY

"I make a doll-baby out of toilet flange wax. They used to be made of beeswax but now they are made of a sticky petroleum wax. I put lots of herbs in the wax, especially Mullein and Black Mustard Seed. Licorice and Calamus are useful if you want to have control over your enemy.

"This doll-baby can be thrown on a fire and it will literally melt away. Brother R.J. James has suggested creating a bed of nails for it by driving nails through a board and putting the doll on the sharp side. I often place the doll in one of the small wooden coffin-shaped boxes you can get at craft stores during the Halloween season. It's great if you want to bury them, but with a few nails driven through, it also makes a convincing iron maiden.

"A doll-baby can be buried in a graveyard, asking a suitable spirit to take care of it, carry it to the devil, or otherwise make the enemy miserable. The spirits of soldiers, policemen, and judges will handle people who have broken the law or acted unjustly. The spirit must be paid so that no debt is incurred by you. I pay with nine dimes and throw them in the hole with the coffin. State your desired outcome to the spirit, make the deal and perform the burial. When done, you should leave and not look back."

NAHNEE'S DEATH DOLL IN A CASKET

This remarkable spell was recorded by Rev. Harry Hyatt in February, 1940, in Algiers, Louisiana. The speaker was a famous rootworker of the time, Nahnee, the Boss of Algiers. What follows is all in her own words.

"To pass a person out, you take a box, like a cigar box or any small box of the kind, and you take that cigar box and you take it to pieces, like it was made, and you cut it as if you was making a casket for a person, but you make it small. Now, you'll make that casket and if it's a white person, you take white silk and you line that box just like a casket is made; if it's a coloured person, you take black or brown silk and line that box.

"Now, you get a doll. It must be a rubber doll. If it's a white person, you get a white rubber doll; and if it's a coloured person, you get one of those brown rubber dolls. And you make coffee, black coffee, for you'll set up all night. You'll take that doll and lay it on a table. If it's a white person you'll write red ink all over that doll — that party's name all over that doll — and if it's a coloured person, you'll use black ink and write the party's name all over the body of the doll, all over, just as many times as you can get it on there. And now you'll dress that doll. If it's a coloured person, you'll dress it up in brown silk or black silk, and if it's a white person, you'll dress it in white silk. And now you'll get perfume and powder and you'll dress that doll's face. If it's a coloured person, you'll get brown powder and you'll dress her face; and if it's white, you'll get white powder and dress her face.

"And you lay that doll out on a table and you make a big pot of black coffee, at night now, about nine o'clock, and you make a pot of black coffee, and you set up there all night with that doll, and you set that pot of black coffee there, and the doll is laid out on the table, the same as if you was holding a wake for a person. You set there over that doll all night, see.

"Now, before sunrise you take that doll off that table and you place that doll into this box that you prepared like a coffin. You place that doll in this box and you cover this box up and you nail this box up with nine brass-head tacks. Before nine o'clock that night you'll find some means to place this coffin under the steps or under the party's house that you done it for.

"Like, if it's you I want to pass out, well, I'll place it under your house or under your steps. You see, this is going to stay under your steps, under your house. I'm going to place it there and it's gonna be there.

"Now you are dead and I done buried you there, you see. Now, just like I buried this doll, well, that's the way they gonna bury you."

CURSING WITH EGGS

BLACK HEN EGG IN A BIRD'S NEST

In October, 1939, Rev. Hyatt interviewed a professional rootworker in Memphis, Tennessee, whose name he lost, and whom he called "Informant 1520." This women taught how to use eggs for cursing.

"You use the bird nest for planting things in it, just like, if you want somebody to die, you take that black Hen's egg and you put it up in there in the bird nest and when the sun dries it up, why, that kills them.

"How do you do it? Well, you take that black Hen's egg and you write the person's name on that egg with ink, and then after writing it on that egg, you run four needles or four long black hatpins through that — two through this way, two through that way. First you put one through one end and one through the other, lengthwise of the egg, and they will cross each other in the middle. Then you go the other way, from side to side. You run the third one through this way, from one side to the other, and you turn it over and run the fourth one through the other way, crosswise. You cross the four of them through that way, to make a cross inside the egg.

"You use a spool of black thread and wrap that up nine times and tie a knot, and nine times more and tie a knot, and keep doing that, nine times and a knot. You wrap it up good and use the whole spool of thread so that nobody can tell it's an egg, and you put that in a bird nest, up in the tree.

"When you do that you're wavering a person's mind — you're running a person crazy. And when that egg dries up, they will die."

A THIRTEEN DAY EGG CURSE

Charles Hanson, an older worker from Georgia, taught Prof. Charles Porterfield this spell: "Take a Black Hen's Egg and with a soft pencil write around the egg in a spiral from top to bottom, writing out what should befall the person you wish to curse, such as, *'John Doe, you have done me wrong and I will see you sicken and die.'* Using a needle that has a broken eye, make a small hole in the top of the egg. Fill this hole with a bit of hair from the person you wish to harm and then seal the hole with wax from a black candle. Every day for thirteen days leave the egg out in the noonday sun and each night set the egg before a lit black candle that is dressed with Black Arts Oil. After the thirteen days finish, take the egg and bury it in a graveyard, walking backwards away from it thirteen steps."

THROW AN EGG INTO RUNNING WATER

In 1937, in Norfolk, Virginia, Rev. Hyatt interviewed Mrs. Mary L. Griffin, an 80 year old midwife and professional root doctor who had been born in slavery in Bertie County, North Carolina, and had lived in Virginia about 50 years. She told him to "Write the person's name on a black Hen's egg and throw it in running water. That sends them away."

In Newport News, Virginia, in 1937, down by the ocean, another worker told Hyatt to use the tides instead of the river's flow: "Write the person's name on a black Hen's egg, throw it into the water as the tide goes out, and soon after, the person will die."

In 1938, in New Orleans, Louisiana, Hyatt received a local variation of the spell: "Take a fresh yard-egg [an egg laid naturally by a free-living chicken], not a grocery egg, and write the person's name on that egg three times. Cross the Mississippi River and when you get in the middle, throw that egg over your left shoulder and you curse it. That breaks their life up."

The same year, another New Orleans practitioner related a variant of this work: "You put a little hole in the shell of a raw chicken egg and suck that raw egg out. Take the person's name and write it nine times, put the name in that egg shell, and stop it up. Throw it in the river, and as long as that egg will float and drift down river, that person will drag. They will just drift through life."

PROFESSOR AMES' EXPLODING EGG SPELL

"Pierce a small hole in both ends and then blow out the contents. Cover one of the holes in the blown-out egg shell with wax or tape and fill the egg with a name paper crossed over with your curses for the person. You can also write out additional cursing on the outside of the egg. Insure that you keep stating your curses when preparing this spell.

"Now, add personal concerns if you have them and fill the rest with herbs and gunpowder. Gunpowder can be purchased from gun stores that have supplies for reloading shells or that serve muzzleloaders. It is also found in firecrackers. Insert a fuse, such as the type you find on bottle rocket type fireworks, and light it. Obviously, observe all safety rules, keeping a distance and avoiding anything flammable nearby. The explosion is pretty sensational. If you don't have an egg, tape your enemy's name paper and a few strands of hair or nail clippings to a bottle rocket and shoot him off into space with a huge explosion."

CURSING WITH THE EVIL EYE

The evil eye, also known as malocchio, bla band, or ayin ha'ra, is mentioned in both the Old and New Testaments. From Middle Eastern origins, it has spread around the world, and as it enters new cultures, beliefs about what it is and who can inflict it vary. Most believe that the evil eye arises as a jealous thought and that it brings about dehydration or death. In most of the world, it is said to be an unintentional side-effect of envy and praise, but in Sicily, it is thought that certain people known as jettatores can project the evil eye. The latter belief has become popular in America, where other names for the projection of the evil gaze are the squint eye, looking cross-eyed, the whammy, and the double whammy.

A long time ago, my best friend, who was a staff physician in a large hospital, had a conflict with a head nurse, who, for some reason, hated him. She would continuously, and falsely, document inappropriate behaviours displayed by him and formally present them to his superiors. The poor guy was constantly being called in by the ethics committee.

One day he had enough. While the nurse was presenting another false incident to the committee, he stared into her eyes and silently commanded that she lose both her mind and her voice every time that she lied. He did this for 10 minutes, without pause. Suddenly, without any prior medical history, the head nurse had a petit mal seizure, a condition she continued to suffer from for decades. The physician had no idea that he had put the whammy on the nurse. But, knowing that I am a witch, he happily called me and told me what he had done. Needless to say, he was elated!

Based on my own personal experiences, this is how to throw the eye:

• Anoint yourself with any type of domination oil.
• Attempt to get as physically close to the enemy as possible.
• Since the eyes are the "windows to the soul," stare into the eyes of your enemy until you feel that you have reached their brain.
• Now, picture a black pool of ink engulfing the enemy's brain.
• Finally, forcefully but silently repeat your command, while visualizing the outcome, as many times as possible. Then, turn away.

For further information about the evil eye see:
LuckyMojo.com/evileye.html by Catherine Yronwode

CURSING WITH FECES

THE FECES TOILET SPELL
Back in the days when people had outhouses instead of indoor toilets, spell-casters would defecate on a piece of brown paper bag, or they would wipe their anus with the paper, and then throw it in the hole with all the other excrement.

As technology has developed, and modernization of waste disposal has evolved, so too has this spell. Now, we are able to not only turn the enemy's life to shit, but also to flush him away. All you need is toilet paper and a pencil or pen. Write your enemy's name on the toilet paper, defecate, wipe yourself with the toilet paper, throw the paper in the toilet, and flush! State your petition as you perform the spell, something like this: *"John Doe, as I shit on you, so will your life turn to shit."* While flushing, you can add, *"John Doe, as your life turns to shit, you will journey into a world of darkness with others who are shit just like you."*

CANDELO KIMBISA'S DOLL BEHIND THE TOILET
Candelo Kimbisa, a professional rootworker in Florida, shares his personal variation of a great old bathroom spell that he learned from Draja Mickaharic. He says, "You make a rag doll out of your enemy's clothing. Preferably you use his dirty underwear. You hide that doll down behind your toilet, on the floor. Every time you piss or shit, that's what he will smell. He will actually be forced to smell shit all the time."

TO PUT THE JINX ON SOMEONE
Cat Yronwode relates this spell by Larry B. Wright: Write your enemy's name diagonally from corner to corner on a square piece of paper, forming an X. Pointing inward from the four center-edges of the paper draw four arrow-shapes. They should point to the place where the names cross. At the center make a small pile of dried powdered Dog shit, Black Pepper, and Gunpowder taken from a bullet or a firecracker. Fold the paper inward from the corners and secure it with thread or string. Hide it in the enemy's yard, house, or place of business to cause bad luck. The smaller you make the packet, the easier it will be to hide.

NAHNEE'S FECES DEATH SPELL

In February 1940, Rev. Harry Hyatt conducted a lengthy interview with a woman known as Nahnee, the Boss of Algiers. This professional hoodoo lady had her own distinctive way of working. Interestingly, although she pulled no punches when it came to cursing, she used the very polite term "passage" to refer to a large, well-formed turd.

"Well, you see, you take the person's passage and you take the person's name. If it's a white person, you take white paper and red ink, and if it's a coloured person, you take brown paper and black ink. You write that party's name all kinda ways, just all over that square piece of paper. You write the name all kinda ways, nine times.

"You take that passage and you sprinkle Cayenne Pepper powder and Black Pepper powder on it, but if it's for a white person you use Cayenne Pepper and White Pepper. You make War Vinegar from vinegar and War Water. That is fighting Pepper and fighting vinegar.

"You add Devil's Shoe String powder and Devil's Dust Powder. You place all that into that passage.

"You take that passage and you wrap it up with thread. See, if it's a white person, you put it in white paper, the big square piece of white paper with the names on it, and you wrap it up and you tie it and wrap it with a whole spool of white thread. But if it's a coloured person, you get the large square piece of brown paper with the names on it and you wrap it up like a package and you wrap it with a whole spool of black thread.

"Now, whilst you wrapping that, you wrap 1, 2, 3, 4, 5, 6, 7, 8, 9, you see, and you wrap that nine times each time. You wrap it with that whole spool of thread, every time you make nine wraps, you make a knot and you wish for what you want done to that person, you see. You make that wish each time you wrap nine wraps. And that is how you wrap that package.

"You take that package and you bury it, see. You bury that package. Now, when that package is buried under the ground, well, this passage dries up, see. This passage, it's buried, you see, and while it's buried all this stuff is gonna commence to working up in there. Everything in there is hot. It's gonna commence to working up, see.

"Now, this party is gonna start to running round like a wild person. He's going crazy. Now, he going crazy, and when this dries up, this passage, when it dries up, this person will pass out.

"That kills him."

CURSING IN FOOD AND DRINK

LIVE THINGS IN YOU

When a worker says that a person was "poisoned," she may be referring to a curse. Often, the poison resides in a contact spell. Being "poisoned through the feet," for instance, may result from stepping into or over Crossing Powder or Goofer Dust.

However, sometimes the magical poison is ingested. In other words, although it is toxicologically inert, eating or drinking a zoological curio may produce magical results. Such ingested poisons are often said to produce "live things in you," the sensation or appearance of small living vermin crawling under your skin, up your legs, or in your abdomen.

- **Frogs:** Eating Frog spawn will cause a person to have "live things."
- **Ground Puppies (Ground Dogs, Mud Puppies):** Gives "live things."
- **Horse Hair:** Swallowing a Horse hair gives the victim "live things."
- **Lizards:** Used the same way that Snakes are, to cause "live things."
- **Snakes:** The eggs, sheds, and skins of Snakes cause "live things."
- **Spiders:** Spider egg cases ("Spider dumplings") cause "live things."

EDIBLE FOODS THAT ARE MAGICAL POISONS

Although it is our secret desire to inflict serious physical harm to our enemies, remember that is it illegal to poison people with toxic substances.

Some cursing herbs and minerals have medicinal or culinary value, while others are toxic. Edible cursing herbs do not have notable cumulative medicinal effects and can be deployed in food or drinks if you state your curse and quote in the name of the target when cooking with them:

- **Asafoetida (Devil's Dung):** To jinx or get revenge on an enemy.
- **Black (Brown) Mustard Seeds:** To cause loss of faith or hope.
- **Black Pepper:** To drive away, expel, and hot foot enemies.
- **Black Walnuts:** To cut away unwanted romantic or emotional ties.
- **Blueberry:** To create sadness, sorrow, or "a blue condition."
- **Grains of Paradise:** Can be used for jinxing (and also for blessings).
- **Poppy Seeds:** To create confusion in mind; to run someone crazy.
- **Red Pepper:** To angrily drive off, send away, and hot foot enemies.
- **Salt:** Essentially protective, it will shield you from enemy attacks.

TRICKY RECIPES TO JINX YOUR FOES

These sneaky recipes come from *Hoodoo Food! The Best of the Conjure Cook-Off and Rootwork Recipe Round-Up* by the Ladies Auxiliary of Missionary Independent Spiritual Church.

TEXAS HOT FOOT CHILI TO DRIVE OFF AN ENEMY

2 pounds grass-fed ground beef (substance)
1 jalapeno pepper, seeded and diced (drive away enemies)
1 serrano pepper, seeded and diced (drive away enemies)
1 poblano pepper, seeded and diced (drive away enemies)
2 cans green chilies, 4 oz. each (drive away enemies)
Gebhardt Chili Powder, to taste (drive away enemies)
1 yellow onion, diced (luck)
2 cloves of garlic, minced (protection)
4 cans Ro-Tel Diced Tomatoes and Green Chilies (female protection)
Turmeric powder, to taste (health, protection)
Cayenne powder, to taste (drive away enemies)
Pinch of black mustard seeds (protection)
Black pepper, ground, to taste, and 13 black peppercorns (protection)
Pinch of salt (protection)

Set stove to medium-high. Sauté peppers, onion, and garlic in a splash of olive oil until peppers are soft and onions are clear. Add ground beef and cook until half done. Add chili powder, spices, tomatoes, and salt. Bring to a boil, then reduce heat to low. Stir counter-clockwise, calling the names of those you want to hot foot and telling them to get the F@#* away from you, out of your life, and out of your business.

Serve hot with cornbread that has been spiked with a dash of cayenne and green chili. Where are the beans? This is Texas chili, and traditional Texas chilis do not have beans. If you can't live without beans in your chili, just add them.

To drive off your enemies and get them to leave you alone, the chili is both spice-hot and stove-hot. However, you also want it to be inviting and tasty. This is great to use at a church potluck or office function. Leave it out anonymously so that your target will eat it.

— Briana Saussy, Texas, MilagroRoots.com

BLACK MAGIC CAKE TO CREATE CROSSED CONDITIONS

1 ³/₄ cup flour (substance)

2 cups sugar (sweetness)

½ cup natural cocoa powder (pleasure)

¼ cup black Dutch process cocoa powder (bitter pleasure)

1 teaspoon baking soda (to rise in power)

1 teaspoon magic baking powder (to rise again)

1 teaspoon salt (protection)

2 eggs from a black hen (accursed energy)

1 cup strong black coffee, brewed (alertness)

1 cup sour milk from a black cow (soured nurturance)

½ cup vegetable oil (the appearance of smoothness)

1 teaspoon vanilla (the semblance of love)

½ cup black walnuts, chopped (to cut away emotional ties)

¼ cup poppy seeds (confusion in mind)

Combine flour, sugar, cocoa, soda, baking powder, and salt in large bowl. Add eggs, coffee, milk, oil, and vanilla. Beat at medium speed for 2 minutes to a thin batter. Fold in black walnuts and poppy seeds until evenly distributed. Pour into greased and floured 13" x 9" x 2" pan. Bake at 350 degrees for 35 - 40 minutes.

Black Magic Cake brings on a confused and crossed condition, concealed by energized excitement. Cocoa, baking powder, and coffee conceal the nefarious poppy seeds that confuse the mind, sour milk that sours the situation, and black walnuts that cross and kill love and luck. Speak your curses as you stir the batter. As it cools, drink hyssop tisane while reciting the 51st Psalm to cleanse yourself. As a precaution, offer cake to the victim anonymously.

— nagasiva yronwode, Yronwode.com
variation on a recipe by Sandy C. Steele
from Bethel Baptist Christian Academy, 1987

The authors of these recipes advise that if you intend to serve either of these enemy tricks at a family or social gathering, you should call the target's name into the food while cooking or baking, to insure the safety of any others who may also partake of the feast.

CURSING THE FOOT TRACK

CROSSING A LIAR WITH PSALMS NUMBER ONE

Catherine Yronwode contributed this spell:

"This basic crossing spell employs foot-track magic to mess up an enemy's life. For the purposes of this example, we will say that the enemy is a liar and a manipulator who has caused a lot of trouble in the neighbourhood. Get the person's picture, write his or her name on it, and cross the name over with your command, such as 'Burn in Hell, you liar.' On the back, copy out the whole of Psalms 1 by hand. This is the Psalm that begins, *"Blessed is the man that walketh not in the counsel of the ungodly, nor standeth in the way of sinners, nor sitteth in the seat of the scornful"* and blesses the righteous man, for *"He shall be like a tree planted by the rivers of water, that bringeth forth his fruit in his season; his leaf also shall not wither; and whatsoever he doeth shall prosper."*

"Wipe fresh, wet dog shit over the paper on both sides. Sprinkle it with Goofer Dust and Red Pepper on both sides. Drop it at the person's doorstep. Over it, in the form of a large X, sprinkle the contents of a whole packet of Crossing Powder. The X should be large enough that your enemy will have to step in, over it, or through it when he or she goes out the door.

"If you are worried that your enemy might recognize your handwriting, be careful! Write the name and the command and the copy of Psalms 1 in block capital letters, very neatly with your 'other hand.' That is, if you are right-handed, write in ALL CAPITALS with your left hand.

"Go home and bathe in weak tea brewed from Hyssop herb and drink a small amount of the tea as well. As you do this, recite Psalms 51 for forgiveness of sin *('Have mercy upon me, O God, according to thy lovingkindness: according unto the multitude of thy tender mercies blot out my transgressions.')*"

GUNPOWDER TO DRIVE AN ENEMY AWAY

This foot-track spell also comes from Cat Yronwode: "Pick up your enemy's left footprint, mix it with Sulphur Powder and Gunpowder, and put the mixture on a piece of brown paper. Light all four corners of the paper with a match and step back. It will blow up and your enemy will be forced to leave town. Another way to do this is to write his name on a paper, lay the paper on his footprint, and shoot the name paper with a bullet."

LIGHTNING STRUCK WOOD IN NINE FOOTPRINTS

In 1937, Doctor Paul Bowles, a professional rootworker in Norfolk, Virginia, shared a foot-track death spell with Rev. Harry Hyatt: "Go to a White Oak tree where the lightning has hit it and collect nine splinters from it. If there is someone you think did something to you, and you can find nine of his foot-tracks, put one of these splinters in each of his tracks, and make a wish that if he did it, the thing will turn back on him and nobody can take it off of him — then, if he did it, he will eventually get down and die."

NINE BURIED NEEDLES, AND HOW TO TURN THE TRICK

Doctor Bowles also had a variant trick, although he warned that it could be turned: "A man can take nine needles and put them point upward under the threshold, the gate, or the house where his victim stays. The victim will walk over them and get sick, and if he doesn't find those needles, they will pin him right down to the bed until he can't get up by himself without help. But if he's wise enough to locate the needles, and he takes them to the river and throws them overboard in running water, then the fellow that did that to him will soon run crazy. He'll have turned this trick back on that man."

FOOT-TRACK DIRT TO RUN HIM CRAZY

In 1939, the Memphis hoodoo lady whom Hyatt called "Informant #1520" said, "If you're going to run somebody crazy or put him to wandering, you pick up the person's left foot-track and you seal it up in a envelope. When you seal that track up, write the person's name on that envelope, and just below it write out the Lord's Prayer, *'Father, Son, and Holy Ghost.'* Go to the river, turn your back to the water, throw that over your left shoulder, backwards, then whirl around and go on home, and they will have to go downstream, in the direction their foot-tracks have gone."

FOOT-TRACKS FOR A JINX, BAD LUCK, AND WANDERING

In 1938, Rev. Hyatt met a 25 year old female card reader and rootworker who had been trained by her family. She told him three foot-track tricks: To put the jinx on an enemy, scoop up his foot-track dirt and sprinkle it around his house in a perimeter circle; he will be made to walk in circles. To give him bad luck but keep him near, pee in his foot-track without moving it. To make him go astray, collect his footprint, place it at the forks of the road, and pee on it; he will be forced to wander to different places.

SPOILED MILK TO RUIN A PARTY

My horrid neighbours planned to have a HUGE party in their front yard. This would have meant an extension of the party into my front yard. A couple of hours before the party, I laid spoiled milk all along our mutual property line, where they would step in it, and demanded that their party be spoiled. Without any meteorological forewarnings (it was predicted to be a beautiful day), a sudden gust of forceful wind came through. This was followed by a sudden drop in temperature and a horrendous rain storm.

It warmed my heart to watch these terrible neighbours frantically move table, chairs, and decorations into their garage, which could barely hold half of their invited guests. The party was a flop!

BLACK PENNY CURSE

Put any strong cursing oil on a penny, state your curse, and throw it on the enemy's property. If they step on it or pick it up, they've touched it.

BROKEN GLASS SPELL

In the Cuban Santeria faith, it is a strict belief that one never picks up broken glass without first having thrown water on it and reciting a blessing from scripture, such as The Lord's Prayer. It is understood that water will wash away any possible curses that have been placed on the broken glass.

Having long believed that this was only practiced in Santeria, it surprised me greatly when I recently witnessed an African-American man smashing a glass bottle on a driveway while screaming his curse that the house's occupant would die once she picked up or walked over the broken glass. The roots of this method of cursing may indeed be African.

H. U. LAMPE'S DEVIL'S OIL WAX BALL FOR REVENGE

Mix something belonging to the enemy with soft wax, form it into a ball, hollow the ball out and carefully fill it with Devil's Oil. Seal it with warm wax and keep it in a safe hidden place for seven days. On the seventh midnight, pierce the ball with a thorn or a needle, and pour the oil into the enemy's footprint, with a curse for justice and revenge, closing with, *"As this oil wastes upon the earth, so may the luck and life of [Name] be wasted on the earth."* A red candle dressed with Devil's Oil and burned on Tuesdays and Saturdays, the days of wrath and justice, can be used to back up this work and continue its effects.

CURSING IN A FREEZER

Since at least the 19th century rootwork practitioners have used blocks of ice and electrical freezers to put enemies and rivals "on ice" and "freeze them out" of activities such as testifying in court, making trouble on the job, gossiping in a church congregation, or interfering with our family and love relationships. In keeping with the traditional nature of this work, animal parts and grocery store items predominate in the creation of these old-fashioned spells.

Freezer spells are only used on enemies. We never freeze our own name or the names of any loved ones for whom we feel any warmth.

BEEF TONGUE TO SHUT SOMEONE UP

This is an old-fashioned court case spell to stop a false witness from testifying, but it can also be used to tie the tongue of any liar.

Spread out a large piece of aluminum foil, shiny side up, and lay a whole Beef tongue on it. Other types of animal tongues may be used, including Lamb, Goat, and Pig. If you inscribe the foil, take care not to tear it. Psalms 109 *("For the mouth of the wicked and the mouth of the deceitful are opened against me")* is highly appropriate for this work.

With a razor blade or knife, carefully make a slit in, but not through, the tongue, starting at the thinner side of the tongue and running about 6 inches toward the thicker side.

On a photo of the enemy, write her name nine times. Turn it to the left, and cross the names with the command "Shut up" written nine times. Add a pinch of Alum powder to it and command the person to shut the fuck up.

If the person is planning to testify in court, add a pinch of Poppy Seed and command that the enemy's testimony will be confusing and garbled. If the person who is planning to testify in court is known to have a bad temper, add a pinch of Red Pepper powder as well, and command that the enemy go crazy with anger, screaming at the judge. Fold the paper away from you, turn it to the left and fold it away from you again. Place it in the center of the cut tongue. Add any personal concerns, if available.

Pour the remaining Alum (and herbs, if you used them) over the contents in the tongue. Pour vinegar over it. Sew the cut shut with black thread. Pound nine coffin nails around the tongue. Wrap the tongue up with thread, then with the aluminum foil. Place it in the freezer and keep it there.

PERMANENT BRAIN FREEZE

Have you ever seen brains at the butcher shop or grocery store and wonder who eats this stuff? Well, luckily for us, some people do and we can take advantage of this.

As with the tongue spell, take aluminum foil and spread it shiny side up on a flat surface. Make several deep cuts into, but not through, the brain. Dissolve a packet of Inflammatory Confusion Bath Crystals in water.

Prepare either one, three, or five petition papers with photos of your victim, or just use petition papers if photos are not available. Write the enemy's name, turn the paper, and cross it with the words, "Mental illness and brain freeze." Empty two vials of dead Red Ants and a packet of Poppy Seeds on the paper and fold it up. If desired, entangle the petition papers with Spanish Moss. Stuff the papers into the several slits in the brain. Follow this with another vial of dead Red Ants and Poppy Seeds. Pour the dissolved bath crystals over the petition papers. Fill any remaining slits with Poppy Seeds and Red Ants.

Sewing the brain shut is not necessary as the meninges of the brain are tightly gathered. Wrap it up in the aluminum foil and freeze it.

KIDNEY FAILURE

One of the most common ailments people get is kidney stones, also known as gravel. To bring on a bout of this painful affliction, obtain an animal kidney. Beef is the easiest to obtain, but any species will do. Dissolve a packet of Destruction Bath Crystals in water, and prepare a number of petition papers with the command, "Kidney Failure." Make several slits into the kidney and fill the slits with small stones of all sizes and wedge in the folded papers. Stab three coffin nails through the kidney. Place the kidney in a container, and fill the container with the dissolved Destruction bath crystals over it. Place the lid on and freeze.

A SHITTY LITTLE CHICKEN-HEARTED NOBODY

To cause an enemy to lose his courage, obtain a Chicken heart, three needles, and fresh Dog feces. Print out a copy of the Three of Swords tarot card, write the enemy's name on it, and around the name write, *"You are a shitty little Chicken-hearted nobody."* Slit the heart open and fill its chambers with feces, wrap it in the copy of the tarot card, and stab the three needles through it as shown on the card. Put it in a glass jar and freeze it.

FREEZE TO DEATH

Dissolve a packet of D.U.M.E. Bath Crystals in water. If you have a photo of your enemy, make the petition over it by writing the name nine times and then crossing it nine times with, "Freeze to death." If you have no photo, just make a name paper, write the petition on it. Fold the paper and stab three coffin nails through it.

Wrap the folded paper tightly in paper towels and place the bundle in a glass jar. Pour enough of the D.U.M.E. Bath liquid over the packet to soak it thoroughly. Seal the jar, leaving enough head space that it will not explode as it freezes. Wrap it up in aluminum foil, shiny side toward the container, and place in the freezer.

MALE IMPOTENCE

Get a Cucumber or a Zucchini, either fresh or pickled, and name it after the man's genitals, saying, *"This is the penis of John Doe."* Place it on a sheet of aluminum foil, shiny side up, and cut a slit into, but not through, almost its full length, leaving about an inch on either side uncut.

The written petition paper command can simply be, "Impotence," or you can use more specific wording, such as, "Your dick is dead and cold." Anoint the petition paper with your victim's semen, if available, and sprinkle it with Saltpeter. Fold the paper up and stuff it inside the vegetable, then add lots more Saltpeter to the inside. Top this off with vinegar, to sour his sex life. Wrap it in the aluminum foil and freeze it.

THIS PUSSY IS SHIT

This spell is to make the vagina of a rival female sexually repulsive to your lover and to prevent the two from having sexual intercourse.

Place a ripe Fig or Pear on a sheet of aluminum foil, shiny side up, and name it after the woman, saying, *"This is the womb of Jane Doe."* Cut a deep horizontal slit into, but not through, it. The petition paper holds the written message, "Your pussy is shit." Anoint the petition paper with her vaginal secretions or menstrual blood and a good amount of dog feces. Fold it up and stuff it into the fruit. Cover the fruit with more dog feces. Wrap it in aluminum foil and freeze it.

For more fantastic freezer spells see this web page:
LuckyMojo.com/freezer.html by Catherine Yronwode

CURSING THE GENITALS

REPRESENTATIONS OF THE PENIS
As we have seen in the freezer spell portion of this book, we can utilize animal parts, fruits, or vegetables to symbolize the body parts of our victims. Here are just a few items we can employ to represent the penis:

- **Pickles**
- **Cucumbers**
- **Zucchinis**
- **Bananas and Plantains**
- **Eggplants**
- **Carrots**
- **Sausages**
- **Salami**
- **Hot Dogs**
- **Popsicles**
- **Cigars**
- **Penis Figural Candles**

HIS LAST BLOW JOB
Mix Goofer Dust, Alum powder, and Blackberry leaves together and then set aside. Next, name and baptize a black or a white penis candle, and inscribe it with the enemy's name and birthdate. Now, talk to the penis very sexily and start sucking it. Tell it how much it wants to fuck. Once you sense that your victim is feeling the sensuality of the blow job, immediately dunk the candle in a large container of ice water. Repeat this process for as long as you feel like having fun with it.

Finally, after the last blow job, bite the very tip of the penis candle off, spit it out, and immediately anoint the candle with Destruction Oil. Then roll the anointed candle in the mixture of Goofer Dust, Alum powder, and Blackberry leaves that was set aside.

Wrap a black cloth around the penis and seal it entirely with duct tape, insuring that there are no visible seams and all that can be seen is duct tape. Now, take the hammer and smash it as often as you please. This can be done every day for a week or in one sitting. After that, run it over with your car. Throw that bastard in a sewer!

COCK TEASE SPELL

Nature Oil enhances the male libido and makes men extremely hot-to-trot, so name and baptize a black or white penis candle and inscribe the victim's name and birthdate on it. Generously anoint the candle with Nature Oil. Begin to manually manipulate the candle, giving it a hand-job. Talk sexily to your victim and tell him how good it feels and that he is just about to ejaculate. Once you sense that he is feeling sexually aroused, stick a heated coffin nail into the candle and scream: *"Suffer, you son-of-bitch!"* Then, wait a few minutes, remove the coffin nail and convincingly apologize to your victim. Promise him that this won't happen again (but, of course, it will happen again!). Repeat this process for as long as desired. When finished, leave the coffin nail in the candle. Dress the candle with D.U.M.E. Oil, roll it in Damnation Incense Powder, and light it. Alternatively, wrap it and crush it as described in the blow job spell.

TAKING HIS MEASURE TO KILL HIS DICK

The "measure" of a man is either the length or the circumference of his erect penis. The length is the more common of the two measures. A thick cotton mop string cut to his measure and smeared with his semen is an intensely sexual link to the man. Once you have his measure, you can tie knots in it to tie his nature for fidelity. Call his name as you start each knot, and when he answers, pull the knot tight.

To give him erectile dysfunction or strangury, dissolve Alum powder, Saltpeter, and Salt in water, and place it in a shallow metal pan. Lay the measure in it and heat the pan, allowing the liquid to dehydrate until a thick crust of the combined salts builds up on the measure. Smear it with fresh Dog feces, sprinkle it with Goofer Dust, put it in a box, and bury it in a graveyard with a little headboard that reads, "Here Lies [Name's] Dick."

THE ROTTING PENIS

Name and baptize a pickle, Cucumber, Zucchini, sausage, or any other perishable representation of the penis. Slice it lengthwise, but do not slice it through, and insert a petition paper, personal concerns, Vandal Root, Devil's Dung, Black Arts Oil, Graveyard Dirt and fresh Dog defecation. Tell the victim that his dick will rot because it looks and smells like shit. Now, wrap it completely in aluminum foil, with the shiny side in. Bury it in the woods to rot away.

REPRESENTATIONS OF THE VULVA AND UTERUS

It is traditional to use animal parts, fruits, or vegetables to represent the body parts of our victims. These items symbolize the vulva and uterus:

- **Avocados**
- **Boiled Cabbage**
- **Cowrie and Conch Shells**
- **Figs**
- **Orchid and Iris Flowers**
- **Oysters, Clams, and Snails**
- **Papayas**
- **Peaches**
- **Pears**
- **Strawberries**
- **Tacos**
- **Vulva Figural Candles**

YEAST INFECTION IN A COWRIE SHELL

Baptize and name a Cowrie shell. Stuff it with personal concerns, a dressed petition for "Yeast Infection," and mouldy bread. Dampen it, wrap it in a black cloth, seal it with duct tape, and bury it in her yard. Keep it moist because yeast infections thrive in a warm, dark, moist environment.

CAT YRONWODE'S "THREE WAYS TO CURSE A PUSSY"

"1. To stop up a woman's fertility, stuff a whole fresh Fig with her name, Red Pepper, Alum powder, and fresh Cat poo, then freeze it.

"2. Put Red Pepper, Alum powder, her pubic hair, and a name paper inside a Cowrie shell. This gives her burning desire but stops up her apparatus. Burn a black vulva candle with her name on it. If the candle is hand-made and the wick is a knotted length of her measure, so much the better. Use the black wax to seal the Cowrie shell. Bury it in her yard.

"3. Here is a very old spell, and it does involve animal death, so beware. Name a living snail for the woman, write her name on its shell, feed it remnants of food she ate, and wrap it in her underwear. Then kill the Snail with Salt, Alum, and Saltpeter. Parch the dead Snail in an oven until dry and grind it to powder. Sprinkle the powder into the woman's food, in her bed, on the chair where she sits, and in the path where she walks."

THE ROTTING UTERUS

Select an Avocado, Papaya, Peach, or Pear. Name and baptize it, then cut it in half, lengthwise, noting that the shape of the interior looks like a human womb. Place a dressed name paper stating that her uterus will rot inside one half and set it aside. Stuff the other half with her personal concerns and two tablespoons of fresh meat or poultry. Put the two halves together and seal the seams with coffin nails, pins, or needles. Wrap a black cloth around it and seal it with duct tape. Set it in an open container outside and let the meat and fruit spoil and rot. When the odour becomes absolutely disguising, throw it in the sewer.

TAKING HER MEASURE TO KILL HER COOCHIE

The "measure" of a woman runs from her clitoral glans to her anus. A cotton mop string cut to her measure and smeared with her fluids is a strong sexual link to her. If you have her measure, you can knot it to tie her nature for fidelity. Call her name at each knot, and when she replies, pull it tight.

To wreck her sex life, dissolve Alum, Saltpeter, and Salt in water, in a shallow metal pan. Lay the measure in and heat the pan until the liquid dehydrates and a crust of the salts builds up on the measure. Smear it with fresh Cat feces, sprinkle it with Goofer Dust, put it in a box, and bury it in a graveyard with a headboard that reads, "Here Lies [Name's] Coochie."

PUCKER UP PUSSY SPELL

Baptize and name an Oyster or Fig. Add a petition paper to "Close the pussy," plus an entire packet of Alum powder. Seal it with black cloth and duct tape. Oysters look like the pussy and are natural aphrodisiacs, so use a generous amount of Alum inside to ensure that these natural properties are annihilated. Bury it on her property.

TARANTULA PUSSY

Name, baptize, and inscribe a vulva candle. With a soldering iron, make a hole in the vaginal entrance and insert pieces of Tarantula exoskeleton (hairy Spider sheds) plus your victim's personal items, vaginal secretions, and measure. Wear gloves when handling Spider sheds, as they are irritating to the skin! Seal the hole with wax. Dress the candle with Crossing Oil, roll it in Destruction Incense, and drive three heated coffin nails into it. Write your curse on her photo. Set the candle on the photo and light it.

CURSING WITH GOOFER DUST

HOW TO USE GOOFER DUST

Goofer Dust is my very favourite cursing powder. It is used to trouble, harm, or to kill an enemy. My successes with Goofer Dust have included one enemy breaking his leg and another breaking his arm. One person was hit by a car. It also caused an entire group of people to hate one another. This is extremely powerful magic!

- As a form of foot-track magic, sprinkle it on the enemy's property. My preference is to make a circle with the dust. Then, put an X inside the circle. Where the two lines meet (center of the X), spit on it after stating the curse and then walk away.
- One old blues song goes, *"Gonna sprinkle Goofer Dust all around your bed,"* so we know it is effective on floors and carpets. It also works well when sprinkled inside the victim's socks or shoes.

GOOFER BALL

Make a ball of black wax, blending into it both Goofer Dust and a piece of the enemy's personal concerns. You may also add mould. Throw it in the yard of the victim. The stated intention of this curse is that disaster will happen to the person who steps on it or picks it up.

LIGHTNING-STRUCK WOOD AND GOOFER DUST

In 1939, "Informant 1520," a hoodoo lady from Memphis, told Rev. Hyatt, "If I wanted something to happen to you, I'd take a splinter out of a tree that lightning has struck and put some of that Goofer Dust on it, and I'd stick it down in the ground by your house, and you will be tormented until you move from there, or your house will be hit by lightning."

STRONG JINX ON AN ENEMY

Cat Yronwode blends Goofer Dust with other curios. "Mix Snake Head herb with Crossing Incense, call your enemy's name, and light it. As it burns, write your enemy's full name backwards nine times in black ink on a sheet of paper that is torn on all four sides. Sprinkle it with Goofer Dust, wrap it around Snake Head herb and Snake shed powder, place the bundle in a raggedly-torn black cloth, and tie it with black thread. Bury the packet in a graveyard and your enemy will get sick."

CURSING WITH GRAVEYARD DIRT

GRAVEYARD DIRT MUSH SPELL
Mix half a packet of Graveyard Dirt with a little Black Arts Oil or Destruction Oil. It ought to have enough consistency to stick to a doorknob or to anything that your enemy touches. Call a curse to make your enemy gravely ill and to carry him to the graveyard, if God wills it.

GRAVEYARD DIRT GET AWAY SPELL
Mix Graveyard Dirt with your favourite cursing oil and a small personal concern of the enemy, such as toenails or hair. Wrap it in black cloth and tie it up with a black thread or string. Bury it far away from the enemy's home so that the enemy will also go far away.

GRAVEYARD DIRT, CRAWFISH, AND SNAKE DUST TO KILL
In Mobile, Alabama, in 1938, a practitioner told Rev. Hyatt how to make a magical poison by mixing together dried and powdered Crawfish dust, Snake dust, and Graveyard Dirt. Add the toenails and fingernails of your victim and regularly sprinkle it where he walks. It will kill him slowly.

THE EMPTY COFFIN
This is my adaptation from a curse by H.U. Lampe.

Make a small coffin of wood, chipboard, or wax. Consecrate it in the names of the Father, Son, and Holy Ghost. No effigy, doll, paper, or personal concern is to be placed within it; it should remain an empty coffin.

Dress two black candles with a mixture of Black Arts Oil and Devil's Oil and put them in matching candle holders. Place the coffin between them, foot toward you, and head away from you. Behind and at the head of the coffin set out a brazier with Double Cross Incense.

Pour Damnation Oil on the coffin. Light the incense first, and then, while you speak your curse, light the black candles. As you continue to curse, slowly sprinkle Graveyard Dirt on the coffin.

Sit in silence and keep watch over the candles until they burn out. This can take from one to six hours. After the flames go out, dress in black and carry the dirt-covered coffin to your enemy's gate or door step, and set it there, foot to his door and head to the street. It is up to you whether you choose do this boldly in daylight, or quietly under cover of darkness.

APOLLO DARK'S GRAVEYARD CURSE SPELL

Apollo Dark says, "This spell is worked in a cemetery, so assemble your ingredients before you set off to do the work. It can be directed against one or more people at the same time, so obtain one or more black male or female figural candles to use as dolls, one for each person to be cursed. In this example, only one candle-doll will be used, but your options are open for more.

"Take your materials to the cemetery and find a grave site that makes you feel comfortable. Introduce yourself and ask the Spirit for assistance with this spell, that is, await a spiritual signal of affirmation or consent. If you receive a sign and still feel comfortable, make three small holes in the grave at the head, heart, and feet. Place a dime in each hole to pay the Spirit, pour a little whiskey over the dimes, and cover the holes with dirt.

"Name, baptize, and inscribe the doll. Anoint it with Crossing Oil. Spread out a sheet of aluminum foil, shiny side upward, and lay the doll on top of it. Pour a little vinegar over it and then start your cursing or prayers, verbalizing aloud what the target did to you to deserve such harsh justice. If desired, you may cause some sort of physical injury to the candle-doll. For instance, you may rip the penis off or stab its eyes, if such harm is warranted by events.

"As you curse, generously sprinkle Sulphur powder over the doll, following with Red Pepper flakes, and spiny Blackberry leaves. Finish by wrapping the candle completely within the foil. Bury it in the grave, about where one of the hands of the deceased person would hold it down. Make sure that it is buried deep enough so that nobody will see it or that weather conditions will expose it."

TO SICKEN AND KILL YOUR SPOUSE

Go to the grave of someone who died of an infectious disease, gather a small amount of dirt there and pay for it with 13 pennies. Take it home and separate it into 13 tiny portions, and as you do so, curse your no-good mate 13 times under your breath, stating everything that he has done to you, saying, for example, *"John Doe, you have sinned against our marriage, and now you will sicken and die by my hand."*

For the next 13 days, sprinkle one portion of the Graveyard Dirt into food that you have prepared for him, being very careful not to eat any of the food yourself.

CURSING WITH INCENSE

USING INCENSE TO BURN CURSING PETITIONS
I always burn self-lighting incense powders on a charcoal disk, within a censer. This allows me to take a petition paper to the Spirit world as quickly as possible with a short, sweet curse.

Lift the charcoal disk with metal tongs, turn it over so the concave side faces down, and light it from below with a flame. Make sure it catches sparks all around. After it ceases to spark, place it in the censer concave side up. When the disk turns grey, place a folded petition paper over it and a layer of cursing incense over the paper. With a lighter or match, light the incense, state your curse, and send your petition to the Spirit world.

DEVIL'S INCENSE TO WRECK A ROOM
Catherine Yronwode describes how to use Devil's Incense to wreak havoc in an area where people will soon be gathering: "If you want to break up a meeting, a political rally, or a job site, just go to the place early, light some Devil's Incense before anyone shows up, call upon the Devils to do their worst, and watch what happens. There will be fussing and fighting, shouting and shoving. In short, unholy Hell will break out."

CAT YRONWODE'S DAMNATION INCENSE CURSE
"Hand-write out Psalms 109, verses 6 - 7 and verses 17 - 19, like so:

> 6. *Set thou a wicked one to be ruler over him,*
>   *And let Satan stand at his right hand.*
> 7. *May he be tried and convicted;*
>   *May he be judged and found guilty.*
> 17. *He loved to curse — May a curse come upon him!*
>   *He would not bless — May blessing be far from him!*
> 18. *May he be clothed in a curse like a garment,*
>   *May it enter his body like water, his bones like oil.*
> 19. *Let it be like the cloak he wraps around him,*
>   *Like the belt he always wears.*

"Smoke the paper in Damnation Incense fumes. If you are bold, address it to your enemy, sign it with your own name, and mail it. If you do not want the person to know what you have in mind, then after smoking it, soak the paper in a liquid which you give to the person to drink."

CURSING WITH MIRRORS

Mirrors are used to reverse injustice or send harm back to evildoers.

BREAK A MIRROR TO GIVE SEVEN YEARS OF BAD LUCK
Dress a picture of your enemy with a cursing oil, place it face-in toward a mirror, and wrap it all in black cloth. At night, take this, with a hammer, to a crossroads. Lay it in the middle of the roads and smash it while calling down seven years of bad luck on your foe. Leave it there and walk away.

REVERSING EVIL WITH ONE MIRROR AND A PHOTO
Use duct tape to affix a photo of your enemy to a mirror, with the picture facing the glass. Write his name backwards on the back, in mirror writing. This can be performed on a bathroom mirror or any small mirror.

REVERSING LIES TO A LIAR WITH TWO FLAT MIRRORS
Print out two small photos of the liar and cut them to fit within the borders of two round compact mirrors. Write the liar's name on the back of each, then glue them back-to-back with the liar's hair between them, making the image "two-faced." Dress the mouths on both sides with Reversing Oil, and sprinkle Red Pepper on them, saying, *"May your lying words burn in your mouth."* Place the double-sided photo between the two mirrors, saying, *"All your lies are reflected back to you."* Seal the edges of the mirrors with duct tape and bury the trick in the liar's yard.

A SMALL MIRROR BOX AND A NAIL-STABBED PHOTO
You will need six small square mirror tiles and duct tape. With two strips of duct tape, sticky side up, make a cross on a flat surface to form the foundation for the box. Lay one mirror, shiny side up, in the middle of the cross of tape. From there, lay one mirror, shiny side up, on each side of the first mirror and one each at top and bottom. Bring each mirror up, along with the duct tape, to form an open box. Run tape around the sides to stabilize the box. Set the sixth mirror, the box lid, aside for now.

Write your curse on the back of your enemy's photo and stab a coffin nail through the photo, right between the eyes. Place the stabbed photo in the box and pour a ccursing oil over it. Close the box with the last mirror tile, and seal it with duct tape. Place it in the freezer or bury it in a cemetery.

MISS CAT'S REVERSING MIRROR-BOX TO FIX BAD WORK

"If you are aware that someone has been trying to cross, goofer, or jinx you, then after you uncross yourself it is a good idea to bind your enemy up in a mirror box spell. The mirror box will keep everything evil they do bouncing back to them, hurting them each time they try to hurt you.

"To work this trick, you will need a doll-baby to represent your enemy.

"Next, get a small box that will just hold the doll. It need be no larger than a shoebox and it can be chipboard or cardboard. It must have a lid. Line it with glued-on shards of broken mirror-glass on which you have written the enemy's name backwards (in mirror writing) before deliberately smashing them. The shards can overlap. Use a sticky glue like Goop. An alternate way to make the mirror box is to get six 4-inch mirror tiles and join five of them together with duct tape to make an open box with all the mirrors facing inward. The sixth mirror is aside to form the lid of the box.

"Working by the light of a black candle that has been dressed with a combination of Uncrossing and Reversing conjure oils, place the prepared doll-baby or effigy in the box and sprinkle it with Red Pepper powder and Sulphur powder or a prepared spiritual sachet powder containing Red Pepper and Sulphur, such as Reversing Powder, Crossing Powder, Revenge Powder, D.U.M.E. Powder, Goofer Dust, or a combination of these. The box can be more intense by first lining it with spiny Blackberry leaves or Cactus pads and adding dead insects or spiders.

"As you sprinkle the sachet powder, say:

"'Here you are, [Name], and here you will stay, and from this time forth, all the crossed conditions you try to bring about, and all the jinxes you try to make, all the foul words that you use, and all the evil that you do will come back to you as these mirrors reflect your image back to you — and in this Hell of your own devising you will burn until God releases you in judgement, Amen.'

"Close up the box, tie the lid down tight with string, carry the 'coffin' to a graveyard, and dig a hole. Ask the spirits in the graveyard to help you hold your enemy down, and as you do so, pay them a dime for their trouble either by throwing it over your left shoulder as you make your request or by placing it at the head of the grave. Bury the box, walk away, and don't look back, going home by a different route than the one you took to get there."

For a further array of reversing spells see this web page:

LuckyMojo.com/reversing.html by Catherine Yronwode

CURSING WITH PLAYING CARDS

In his classic book, *A Deck of Spells: Hoodoo Playing Card Magic*, Professor Charles Porterfield teaches these deadly cartomantic curses:

FOUR OF SPADES: SICKEN A FOE

"To sicken an enemy, take a Four of Spades and draw a line between the top two Spades and a line between the bottom two Spades, making the headboard and footboard of a bed. Write your foe's name in the middle of the card, and 'HERE You Stay' beneath it. Dress the card and four black candles with Black Arts Oil and Graveyard Dirt.

"After midnight, while the hands of the clock are going down, and your foe is in their bed, place one candle on each of the four Spades, making bedposts, and light them. As the candles burn call out to your foe in a whisper, telling them that they shall no longer rest easy or rise from their bed in health, and shall stay in their bed sick. When done, take the card and any leftover wax and bury it in the graveyard or behind a hospital."

ACE OF SPADES: DEATH UNTO MY ENEMIES

"If you have a justified cause to create trouble, pain, or even death for an enemy, take an Ace of Spades and write the enemy's name on it nine times. If the enemy is unknown use a title: 'My Enemy' or 'The God Damned Traitor.' Then write a destructive command, such as 'Die a Painful Death' or 'Waste Away and Go,' from one corner of the card diagonally to the opposite corner, and again between the other two corners, so that the two commands form an X on the card. Dress, tape, or tie personal concerns such as hair, menstrual blood, semen, a photo, or a business card from the enemy to the Ace of Spades. Place seven needles, whose eyes you have broken with a pair of pliers, into a black candle to mark off seven sections, dress it with D.U.M.E. Oil, and then place it on top of the card.

"During the waning moon, when the hands of the clock are falling, light the candle and burn one section each day for seven days. Pour more D.U.M.E. Oil on the candle each day, and snuff it out between burns.

"When the work is done, collect the card, needles, and any remaining candle wax and wrap them in black cloth, tying it all up with black thread. Take the wrapped package and dispose of that mess at a crossroads, into a river, or, better still, bury it in a graveyard."

JACK OF SPADES: CATCH AND KILL AN ENEMY'S LUCK

"To rob an enemy of their luck and then kill that luck, take the Jack of Spades from a new deck of cards and write the name of the one whose luck you wish to catch and kill on the top of the card and 'Hangman, Ketch Their Luck' on the card's foot. Get two coffin nails, dress them with Jinx Oil, and pin them through the card at the Jack's hands so that he is 'holding' them. Tape a few Black Cat hairs to the card, and place it under a black candle dressed with Jinx Oil and a pinch of Graveyard Dirt. Make up a mixture of equal parts Vandal Root and Walnut leaves, burn it over live charcoal, light the black candle, and call out over the burning candle:*'Hangman, ketch [the target's name's] luck and kill it now! So, that all they try to do will come to nothing!'*"

TAROT CARDS FOR CURSING

Here are some "bad luck" tarot cards that can be used for cursing.

Find these images from the public domain Rider-Waite-Smith tarot deck online and print them out about six or seven inches high, in colour. Use them as labels to glue onto the glass holders of black vigil light candles.

If you are creative with scissors and paste or know how to use digital photo-editing applications, insert your enemy's face in place of the face of the one who is suffering in each of these cards. Select several images to create your own personal narrative of intent, then light one daily.

- **The Hanged Man (XII):** A traitor being punished. Self-undoing.
- **Death (XIII):** Death conquers all whose names are called.
- **The Devil (XV):** Abuse. Domination. Addiction. Bondage.
- **The Tower (XVI):** Danger, Destruction. Heaven's rightful wrath.
- **The Moon (XVIII):** Fear of the unknown. Confusion. Mental Illness.
- **Three of Swords:** Heart attack. Cheating. Three forms of sorrow.
- **Four of Swords:** Illness leading to a slow death. Put on ice.
- **Five of Cups:** Disappointment. Loss. The haunted past. An old curse.
- **Five of Pentacles:** Homeless. Unnatural Illness. Unable to get help.
- **Five of Wands:** Anxiety. Open conflict. Struggles within a group.
- **Eight of Swords:** Bound and tied up. Powerless. Helpless. Alone.
- **Nine of Swords:** Insomnia. Anxiety attack. Depression. No bed-mate.
- **Ten of Wands:** Burdens. Oppression. Failure to achieve a goal.
- **Ten of Swords:** Destruction. Despair. Betrayed by multiple enemies.

CURSING WITH PRAYERS

LEARN TO PRAY WITH CONVICTION

Formal prayers are a type of invocation, and they should be recited with thought, passion, and vision. Envision what you are reciting. If you are calling on a Saint, envision the Saint's presence. Feel that entity around you or in front of you. The content of the prayers also ought to be envisioned. Let's employ verses from Psalms 23 as an example:

Verse 5: *"Thou preparest a table before me in the presence of mine enemies: thou anointest my head with oil; my cup runneth over."*

I see myself sitting at a table while my enemies stand and watch. There is a cup in front of me, filled to the very top, with water. Then, God comes to me, smiling, and anoints my head with Holy Oil while my foes just stand and wallow in their envy.

My verbal requests or petitions are followed by pleas of passion, as a child begs a parent for assistance. Many rootworkers maintain that if we beg God or the Saints, they will respond with the love and pity that a parent would for their own flesh-and-blood child. And, as a result, they will feel compelled to help us.

CALL UPON YOUR SPIRITUAL COURT

You have a spiritual court consisting of those upon whom you can call for assistance as you curse. Just to name a few, you could summon:

- **God Almighty, the Lord, the Divine**
- **The Angels and Archangels of Heaven**
- **Your Guardian Angels**
- **Figures from the Bible, according to their history and your need**
- **Catholic Saints, according to their patronage**
- **The Deities of religions not your own (but be careful with these)**
- **Your Spirit Guides**
- **Your Ancestors from time immemorial to those recently deceased**
- **Deceased friends who understand your need and wish to help**
- **Deceased people who once were soldiers, judges, or policemen**
- **Animal Spirits, domestic or wild, known or unknown**
- **Wild Spirits such as Fairies, Trolls, Goblins, Nixies, or Sirens**
- **Imps, Devils, Demons, and Satan (but be careful with these)**

WHAT TO SAY OR WHAT TO PRAY

No matter whom you call upon to help you, an explanation or reason for your curse is always verbalized. This serves a three-fold purpose:

- **It justifies our work:** We explain our need to the entities.
- **We receive their pity:** Therefore they grant more forceful assistance.
- **It reminds us of our hurt and anger:** This anger can then be more vividly conveyed into our work.

Calling in Spirits is pretty easy. I just call them three times, out loud, and ask them for assistance. Here is an example of what I may say:

"I call upon my Spirit Guides! I call upon my Spirit Guides! I call upon my Spirit Guides! I ask for your assistance with this spell to curse John Doe, as he has been cruel to me and to my family. He poisoned my beloved dog, he beat up my child, and he threatened to kill me. Now I seek revenge for all the pain that he has caused."

Other people use a different, but equally common form of prayer, not unlike what you might hear in church:

"Lord, I come to you tonight with a heavy heart and head bowed down, asking for an end to the suffering caused to us by John Doe, an unrepentant sinner. Lord, this man has been cruel to me and to my family, He poisoned my beloved dog, he beat up my child, and he threatened to kill me. Lord, as you granted revenge and victory to King David when his enemies beset him, so I now seek righteous vengeance for all the pain that this man has caused, and I ask you for complete and utter victory over him in every way, until he goes down to a speedy, unmourned death. In Jesus' name, Amen!"

When I am repeatedly jabbing, stabbing, or beating an effigy, I will scream my curses at my foe. It may go something like this:

"Feel the pain that you caused me, you son-of-a-bitch! You will be destroyed, destroyed, DESTROYED! John Doe, at my hands, you will suffer! Suffer! SUFFER. Go to Hell, you BASTARD!"

7 DEADLY BIBLE PSALMS TO QUELL YOUR ENEMIES
By Catherine Yronwode of HoodooPsychics.com

Even religiously-minded people have enemies, suffer oppression, and need relief from cruelty. God has inspired some very serious prayers, in the form of Psalms, which can be recited while casting justified curses. Known as the "imprecatory Psalms," these prayers are powerful, effective, and definitely not to be trifled with!

- **Psalms 1:** This Psalm removes unworthy and ungodly people from any group. Key phrases: *"The ungodly [...] are like the chaff which the wind driveth away [...] the way of the ungodly shall perish."*
- **Psalms 37:** This cursing Psalm invokes physical injury and brings death by sword and fire to evil people. Key phrases: *"The arms of the wicked shall be broken [...] their sword shall enter into their own heart [and] the wicked shall perish [...] as the fat of lambs [...] into smoke shall they consume away."*
- **Psalms 55:15:** Here is a simple, direct, and right-to-the-point destruction Psalm. What's more, it asks God to give your enemies no warning, but to kill them unawares. Key phrases: *"Let death take my enemies by surprise; let them go down alive to the grave."*
  Psalms 58:6: Talk about specialized curses! This Psalm sends your enemies — especially gossipers, liars, and false tale-bearers directly to the dentist! Key phrases: *"O God, break the teeth in their mouths."*
- **Psalms 59:12:** God really hates liars, and this Psalm asks for particular curses to fall upon those who lie with arrogance, pride, or use foul language. Key phrases: *"For the sin of their mouth and the words of their lips let them be taken in their pride: and for cursing and lying which they speak."*
- **Psalms 109:8:** Do you need to remove a bad politician or government official from your life? This is the Psalm to do it! Key Phrases: *"Let his days be few and let another take his office."*
- **Psalms 137:9:** Finally, here is a terrible curse of vengeance that draws down God's ire upon entire families and employs military means to do so. Be careful with this one, folks — it's scary! Key Phrases: *"How blessed will be the one who seizes your infants and dashes them against the rocks!"*

CURSING WITH SALT

THROWING SALT
Throw salt at the person's back as they walk away and state your curse. I usually say, *"Break a leg, you son-of-a bitch!"*

If the enemy is driving away, throw the salt behind the car and scream, *"Get into a car accident, you son-of-a-bitch!"*

Not only are these old hoodoo curses, they are also an old Cuban curses, rooted in the brujeria tradition that my Mother taught me.

A SALTED CURSE IN YOUR SHOE
Write out a curse, stuff it with salt, fold it, and put it in your shoe. Every time that you walk on that paper, your enemy will feel the effects.

BROOM AND SALT TO SEND A FOE OUT OF YOUR HOUSE
If an enemy is visiting and you want her to leave, turn a broom upside-down while she is in your home. This will give her a feeling of uneasiness and she will want to leave earlier than had been planned. As she is leaving, throw a few handfuls of salt on the floor behind her. Then, when she is out of hearing range, sweep the salt right out the door by which she left, while calling your curse out loud. This is concluded by picking up the broom and shaking it, as violently as possible, while continuing to curse her.

A simpler variation of this spell uses no salt, just a broom. All you do is sweep the floor behind your enemy as she is leaving. But be careful, this is a well-known hoodoo curse and many will be aware of your intention. All your foe has to do to break this jinx is to simply spit on the broom.

BATH SALT CRYSTALS FOR A CAR ACCIDENT
One of my very favourite ways of promoting a car accident is to spray the enemy's car, and especially the door handle, with Destruction Bath Salt Crystals dissolved in water. Remember, though, that cursing bath crystals have a distinct odour, so you will need to become familiar with the odour and decide what amount could be detectable. If you make a well diluted mixture, the scent will either go unnoticed or it will be mistaken for rain, a dirty car passing by, or kids playing near the vehicle. When petitioning for such a justified curse, please ask that the car accident not injure any innocent bystanders or occupants of the car.

CURSING IN A SWEET GUM TREE

These old, rural curses make use of a living tree as a "container." They were published by Catherine Yronwode in *Hoodoo Herb and Root Magic:*

TO CAUSE AN ENEMY FOOT PAIN

"Cut a piece from the toe and a piece from the heel of your enemy's sock or stocking. Sprinkle them with Red Pepper, and stab them together with nine sewing pins. Go into the woods, bore a hole in a Sweet Gum tree, and put the pieces in. Cut a plug from a branch of the same tree and plug the hole. As the tree grows over the plugged hole, your enemy's feet will swell up."

TO GET SOMEONE TO LEAVE YOU ALONE

"Pick up the bothersome person's going-away foot-track, heel to toe, bottle it, and hang it from a Sweet Gum tree. As the cord twists and untwists, he will become mentally uncertain; when the cord breaks, he will go."

TO SOUR AN ENEMY'S LIFE

"Soak your enemy's hairs, fingernails, toenails, and nine pins in vinegar for nine days. Before sunrise of the tenth day, bore a hole in a Sweet Gum tree and put the items in the hole. Cut a plug from the tree, dip it in the vinegar, and give it two light taps to set it. Every morning before dawn give it two more taps. On the ninth morning, drive it in. This will sour his life."

TO STOP UP SOMEONE'S BOWELS

"Knead Red Pepper powder into your enemy's feces, tightly pack it in a small glass bottle, and cork it. Bore a hole in a Sweet Gum tree, slip the bottle in, stop it up with a peg cut from the same tree, then cut the peg off smoothly. As the tree grows over the peg, your enemy will be troubled with abdominal pain, cramping, constipation, or obstructions of the bowels."

TO STOP UP A WOMAN'S BLOOD

"Get a piece of a woman's used menstrual pad, tampon, or blood-soiled underwear, carry it into the woods before sunrise, bore a hole in a Sweet Gum tree, pack it into the hole, and carve a peg from the same tree. Every morning, tap the peg into the hole; on the ninth morning drive it in. She will have painful periods or stop menstruating. Add Graveyard Dirt, and she may die."

CURSING WITH WAR WATER

In the space of two weeks in 1938, Harry Hyatt interviewed six workers in Mobile and New Orleans who each used War Water a different way:

RUN THEM OFF WITH WAR WATER AND SPICES
February 26, Mobile: Put Salt, Black Pepper, Cinnamon, and Cloves into a bottle of War Water. Pour it on a family's front steps to run them off.

YOU CAN CROSS A HOUSEHOLD UP WITH WAR WATER
February 26, 1938, Mobile: Make the sign of the cross on your enemy's door with chalk. Go buy a bottle of War Water, come back and pour it on the cross to cause disagreeableness, confusion, and fighting in the house.

WAR WATER AND GUINEA GRAINS WILL MOVE HER OUT
March 2, 1938, New Orleans: Powder a packet of Guinea Grains and put the powder into a bottle of War Water. Go to your enemy's house when she is away, stand with your back to the house, throw the bottle backwards to break it on the wall, and walk away. She will move out.

FOOT-TRACK DIRT IN WAR WATER MAKES HIM ROVE
March 11, 1938, New Orleans: With your right hand, take dirt from the heel to toe of a person's right foot-track. Put it into a bottle of War Water, seal the bottle, and throw it in the Mississippi River. The person will not be able to hold a job, will go from town to town, and will have a roving mind.

WAR WATER MAKES THEM LEAVE TOWN OR GO TO JAIL
March 11, 1938, New Orleans: Get War Water from the drug store, pass by your enemy's house at night and throw it at the porch as you say a curse for them to move out or go to jail, and they will move or go to jail.

EVAPORATED WAR WATER TURNS HIM INTO A DRIFTER
March 12, 1938, New Orleans: Pick up your enemy's foot-track, put it in a dish, and pour a bottle of War Water onto it. Let the War Water evaporate until the dirt is dry, then take the dirt to the Mississippi River and throw it backwards over your left shoulder into the channel of the river. As it goes downstream, your enemy will keep drifting downward all his life.

CLEANING UP AFTER CURSING

RETURNING TO THE WORLD REFRESHED

Cursing, if done with true intensity and in justified wrath, is quite a journey. We have gone from victimhood to vengeance — and now it is time to turn back from that path, to return to the mundane world and to our spiritual homes in peace. We have called up negative Spiritual forces, energies, and even entities, and they now inhabit our work spaces and ourselves. Therefore, it is vital that we draw a close to our cursing by cleansing our work spaces with Chinese Wash, followed by spraying the areas with Florida Water.

Additionally, I like to light either Tibetan Ghost Purging Incense or Uncrossing Incense on a charcoal disk. I close all the windows, and smoke each room with the incense. This acts as "spiritual tear gas" for any evil spirits who wish to keep hanging around. What is the normal reaction to tear gas? Escape! They want to get out! So, after having attacked them with incense, I open one window and door at a time and demand that all unpleasant entities exits immediately — and they will gladly do so!

Next comes the personal cleaning.

Like many others, I use Hyssop herb to cleanse myself. In addition to eradicating negative energies, Hyssop aids us with asking God for forgiveness and atonement for any acts of wrongdoing, as prescribed in Psalms 51. This is not to say that cursing itself is wrong — but if you have gone overboard and cursed someone who did not deserve your ire, such as a child or a person who you have learned was innocent of wrongdoing, Hyssop is prescribed to wash away your errors.

Make a mild tea of Hyssop herb. Light two white 4" or tea light candles dressed with Uncrossing Oil. Place one to each side of your shower or at the head and foot of your tub. As you stand in the tub or shower stall, recite the 51st Psalm, drink a few sips of the Hyssop tea and use the rest of it to wash your body downward, ending with the soles of your feet. Sincerely and contritely ask for forgiveness if you placed your curse in error. Leave your bath by walking between the two white candles. Air dry and anoint your body lightly with Blessing Oil, from the feet upwards.

For more information on the use of Hyssop see:

Herb-Magic.com/hyssop.html

FREQUENTLY ASKED QUESTIONS

The Lucky Mojo Forum was established in 2008. Averaging 71 posts per day, it is an online community in which questions are answered about the practice of hoodoo and the use of Lucky Mojo spiritual supplies. To date, there have been 211,500 posts on 14,500 topics about hoodoo!

The Forum community, which consists of 12,500 members, is a loving, caring, thoughtful, and extremely intelligent group of people whom I consider to be my Lucky Mojo Forum Family Members. At this wonderful place, we all teach each other as well as learn from each other on a daily basis. The Forum is open to all and we would love to meet and converse with you there. So, please, come join our family! The Lucky Mojo Forum is free to join and can be accessed online at:

Forum.LuckyMojo.com

In 2014, it was my honour to be appointed an Administrator of the Lucky Mojo forum. To date, I have written more than 14,200 posts in response to a variety of questions regarding the spiritual practices of conjure and rootwork.

Other answers to questions are provided by regular Forum members and by a dedicated team of Moderators, all of whom are graduates of Catherine Yronwode's Hoodoo Rootwork Correspondence Course.

Read more about the Hoodoo Rootwork Correspondence Course at:

LuckyMojo.com/mojocurse.html

When reading the answers to the questions provided in this book, please note that usernames followed by an (M) are people who are or were at one time Forum Moderators. Those marked (M, AIRR) are Moderators who are also in professional practice as members of the Association of Independent Readers and Rootworkers. In addition to myself, those whose replies are printed here are:

Catherine Yronwode   **Conjureman Ali**
Devi Spring   **Lukianos**

All AIRR members can be reached for personal readings, rootwork, magical coaching, custom spell-casting, and related professional services at the AIRR web site:

ReadersAndRootworkers.org

• I spilled Hot Foot Powder on my altar!

How do I clean up the Hot Foot Powder on my altar? Will it hurt me?
— ttoobbyy

Hot Foot Powder has a purpose — it is not a rogue element that can take over and control your altar space. Think: We make it in the shop and we are still here. Your will and prayers are important. Spiritual supplies do not operate on their own — they are engaged as tools. Chinese Wash is easy to use as a cleaner when diluted with water.
— catherineyronwode (M, AIRR)

• Can I give payback to unknown people by burning a candle?

Is there a candle to give everyone who in the past few years has caused you grief a payback? I am not even sure who all caused the grief. Sometimes it's the people who smile to our faces who stab us in the back.
— suzyparker

If you do not even know the names of the people, then I would say that one candle won't change them, and it's not worth it: that is life. People are going to send negativity your way, spread rumours, gossip about you, and so on. Just think of those people as lessons in your life. Learn from them and move on. I am not saying that those people had the right to do that to you, but dang, if I went back and tried to get back at every single person since I came out of the womb that talked ill of me, I would be wasting my energy, time, and money on people that aren't even worth it!
— starinthesky (M)

• Should I do cleansing work while working a black poppet doll?

Is it necessary to do a cleansing bath when doing black work using a black poppet doll? If so, how frequently does one need to do the cleansing?
— mabel

Protect yourself before negative works and cleanse yourself afterward.
– Lukianos (M, AIRR)

• If you lay down tricks, can you trick yourself?

I have a mailman who is causing trouble with our house and dogs. I have rubbed oils on the mailbox where he would touch. I laid down Hot Foot powder where he would walk. Can I accidentally work against myself or others who might touch the mailbox or cross this path?
— ShadoWalker

No. I was always taught that if you have an enemy in mind to lay down powders while calling that person into it. For example, *"Mr Mailman, as you walk into this mess, may your feet burn until you run out of town."*
— Conjureman Ali (M, AIRR)

• Can a D.U.M.E. spell hurt me if I did it without justification?

In my D.U.M.E. candle petition, I asked for a couple to separate and then die horrible deaths. I've since had strµong, powerful spiritual messages and "warnings." My boyfriend said if I didn't sort myself out, he would leave me. My partner spoke of suicide tonight. It's just all too much. I feel numb, like I've had a warning from God himself that he is angry with me for wishing bad things on this couple. I want to ask for forgiveness.
— Nony65

Given these signs, the right thing is to start cleansing and protection work, in that order. Praying that a couple "die horrible deaths" is pretty damn heavy work; if it wasn't justified in the eyes of God, you could be feeling the heaviness of that sin. And if your partner is serious about the suicide talk, get him help immediately. Hang in there!
— SisterJean (M)

• Which cursing oil is strongest?

Crossing, Black Arts, Devil, and Destruction oils: Which is strongest?
— sun369

None is inherently stronger than another; they each have different aims.
— Turnsteel

How do I recover from what I've done?

I just got really crazy and devastating news. My ex's new girlfriend passed away. He came back from a trip and found her in his bed. It sounds like suicide. I did work to break them up and for him to feel pain, but NEVER this. I feel truly awful …

Please be careful with this work … things like this can happen when you are inexperienced and fuelled with hate and a need for revenge. I deeply regret the work that I did now. I need to make amends with her spirit now. I didn't know her and I never wanted to hurt her. She had three kids. I just feel awful. I lit a candle for her last night and prayed the rosary for her. It felt good to connect with her that way. I have the feeling she was a very pure hearted, but broken person … I can't stop thinking about her. I don't know how I'm going to recover from what I've done.

— littlewing

As a Catholic, I know that the Priest gave you penance. So, that ought to clear you. As far as the psychological aspect of guilt, I'm not a therapist but I suspect that time will heal your wounds. However, cursing is a serious matter and you may want to talk to a professional medical person if you just can't get over this. Also, work on some healing spells for yourself: LuckyMojo.com/healing.html. We love you, littlewing!

— Miss Aida (M, AIRR)

Cleansing prayer needed after doing harmful tricks?

I just did a vinegar jar spell to break up my ex and his other babymom. Now I hear I need a cleansing prayer to say after every time I shake my jar. Any suggestion on cleansing prayers that work well?

— cluv87

You should absolutely be doing cleansing work for yourself. I recommend that you use Hyssop herb tea to cleanse yourself while praying Psalms 51. Complete the task properly by physically bathing yourself with Hyssop, while praying. Hyssop is the Biblical herb that specifically cleanses away sin, that is, negative energy that you generate yourself.

— Devi Spring (M, AIRR)

CONCLUSION

Approaching the end of this book is a bittersweet moment for me. I feel gratified that I have been able to share so much, yet, on the other hand, I am sad that it is indeed coming to a close. I hope that you've enjoyed reading this book as much as I have enjoyed writing it. Thank you, each and every one of you, for joining me on this journey.

Before we part, please bear in mind that knowledge is power. You have been given a lot of knowledge, so please be prudent when performing these spells. Please make sure that you are justified. Do not abuse your power!

Many years ago, as a teenager, I was fortunate to receive karate lessons from a private group of Okinawans. Because I was the youngest student, these masters gave me special attention and insured that things were explained to me numerous times. They taught me how to defend myself and they taught me easy ways to kill an attacker ... but they also embedded into my brain, over and over and over again: *"You have the knowledge and ability to kill. Do not abuse your power. If a person starts a fight with you, walk away or run away. You have nothing to prove. Nothing!"*

Running away is what I did. Yes, I looked like a coward but it was a lot better than the alternative — causing severe injury or death.

Once, a relentless bully just would not stop picking on me. I kept running away until I acquired the reputation of being a spineless, gutless idiot. Inevitably, the bully cornered me outside, with a crowd of others encircling us. As the bully's fist was approaching my abdomen, it only took one swift karate move to bring this monster down — with severe injuries. But although I was the victor in the eyes of many, guilt consumed me.

Guilt is a common consequence of causing injury to others. Many of us do not consider the possible consequences when we are angry. This is why I leave you with a warning: It is imperative to think about the damages that a negative spell will impose on another. So, pause before taking action! You now have the knowledge and ability to get revenge but, please, be prudent! Be justified! Do not abuse your power!

If you need my help, there are many places to find me — my web site, the Lucky Mojo Forum, AIRR, or Hoodoo Psychics. My web address is:

MissAida.com

May you be victorious in all your battles.

BIBLIOGRAPHY

DE CLAREMONT, Lewis. *Legends of Incense, Herb, and Oil Magic*. Oracle Publishing, 1936; Lucky Mojo Curio Co., 2016.

GARDBACK, Johannes. *Trolldom: Spells and Methods of the Norse Folk Magic Tradition*. The Yronwode Institution for the Preservation and Popularization of Indigenous Ethnomagicology (Y.I.P.P.I.E.), 2015.

THE HOLY BIBLE, King James Version, Rev. Edition, Thomas Nelson, Inc., 1976.

HASKINS, JIM. *Voodoo and Hoodoo*. Scarborough House Publishers, 1978; Stein and Day, 1978.

HYATT, Harry Middleton. *Hoodoo – Conjuration – Witchcraft – Rootwork*. [Five Vols.] Memoirs of the Alma Egan Hyatt Foundation, 1970–78.

HURSTON, Zora Neale. *Mules and Men*. J.B. Lippincott, 1935. Reprinted, Harper Collins, 1990.

LaFÆ, Miss Phoenix. *Hoodoo Shrines and Altars: Sacred Spaces in Conjure and Rootwork*. Lucky Mojo Curio Co., 2015.

LAFOREST, Aura. *Hoodoo Spiritual Baths*. Lucky Mojo Curio Co., 2014.

LAMPE, H. U. [Pseud. of Larry Bernard Wright]. *Famous Voodoo Rituals and Spells*. Marlar Publishing, 1974.

MICHÆLE, Miss and Prof. Charles PORTERFIELD. *Hoodoo Bible Magic*. Missionary Independent Spiritual Church, 2014.

MICKAHARIC, Draja. *A Century of Spells*. Samuel Weiser, 1988.

----------. *Spiritual Cleansing*. Samuel Weiser, 1982.

LADIES AUXILIARY OF MISSIONARY INDEPENDENT SPIRITUAL CHURCH. *Hoodoo Food! The Best of Conjure Cook-Off and Rootwork Recipe Round-Up*. Missionary Independent Spiritual Church, 2014.

LEFÆ, Phoenix. *Hoodoo Shrines and Altars*. Missionary Independent Spiritual Church, 2015.

MAYFIELD CLINIC. *Anatomy of the Brain*. MayfieldClinic.com

PORTERFIELD, Professor C. D., *A Deck of Spells, Hoodoo Playing Card Magic in Rootwork and Conjure*. Lucky Mojo Curio Co., 2015.

RIVA, Anna, *Spellcraft, Hexcraft and Witchcraft,* International Imports, Inc., 1977.

TOWELHEAD, Troll [The Grand Mufti of Satanism]. *The Gospel of Satan with Commentary and Selected Fatwas*. Scholomance Press, 2013.

YRONWODE, Catherine. *Hoodoo Herb and Root Magic: A Materia Magica of African-American Conjure*. Lucky Mojo Curio Co., 2002.

----------. *Paper in My Shoe: Name Papers, Petition Papers, and Prayer Papers in Hoodoo, Rootwork, and Conjure*. Lucky Mojo Curio Co., 2015.

----------, et al. *The Black Folder: Personal Communications on the Mastery of Hoodoo*. Missionary Independent Spiritual Church, 2013.